"As you devour this fresh book by our dear friends, your senses will be enlivened and even overloaded! You will end up empowered by the Holy Spirit to do what Jesus does. This book is raw and contagious. Only one thing is lacking: a warning sign that says, 'Your life will change when you read this book!' We highly commend to you the life and writings of Heidi and Rolland Baker."
—**James W.** and **Michal Ann Goll**, Encounters Network and Compassion Acts

"Heidi's stories of Jesus meeting the needs of the poor will make us jealous to be part of the answer for a dying, sick world. Read of miracles and those who are not afraid of getting involved with dirty hands and broken hearts."
—**Jackie Pullinger**, director, St. Stephen's Society, Hong Kong

"Only eternity will reveal the impact of the laid-down lives of the Bakers. Not only have they started a revival that has changed the continent of Africa, but they are training hundreds of eager 'others' to do it as well. How, you ask? By enjoying and expecting miracles *now*!"
—**John Arnott**, senior pastor, Toronto Airport Christian Fellowship

"I consider Heidi and Rolland Baker to be world missionaries, profoundly impacting not only a nation but the whole world. This book is a graphic statement of how to do missions, as their 'missiology' in Mozambique is the loudest and clearest statement of how to reach the world by supernatural means. Every missionary, every missions strategist from every mission board and everyone interested in world missions should consider *Expecting Miracles* a must-read. There are many great mission stories from the past worth reading, but this one is taking place as we speak—right now! Read it, weep and become involved!"
—**Jack Taylor**, Dimensions Ministries, Melbourne, Florida

"Heidi and Rolland Baker are great role models who are writing a contemporary book of Acts. I have had the privilege for almost ten years of knowing them as close friends and of having worked alongside them in Africa, Europe and North America. They walk with a contagious passion for Jesus and an equally contagious compassion for the hurt, lost

and poor. The Bakers are continually being used by God to give out the bread of life from their own deep and abiding intimacy with God. This book will inspire many toward living a sacrificial, Christlike lifestyle."
—**Marc A. Dupont**, Mantle of Praise Ministries, Inc.

"Both Jesus and James said, 'Faith without works is dead.' You will weep and praise as you read this current anthology of frontline stories powered by the Holy Spirit in the name of Jesus."
—**Darrel Eldridge**, director of administration, Iris Ministries

Expecting Miracles

True Stories of God's Supernatural Power and How You Can Experience It

Heidi and Rolland Baker

Grand Rapids, Michigan

Published by Chosen Books
A division of Baker Publishing Group
P.O. Box 6287, Grand Rapids, MI 49516-6287
www.chosenbooks.com

Originally published under the title *The Hungry Always Get Fed: A Year of Miracles* by New Wine Ministries of West Sussex, England

Third printing, January 2011
Printed in the United States of America

Library of Congress Cataloging-in-Publication Data

Baker, Heidi.

Expecting miracles : true stories of God's supernatural power and how you can experience it / Heidi and Rolland Baker.

p. cm.

ISBN-13: 978-0-8007-9434-7 (pbk.)

ISBN-10: 0-8007-9434-6 (pbk.)

1. Baker, Heidi. 2. Baker, Rolland. 3. Missionaries—Mozambique—Biography. 4. Church work with children. 5. Miracles. I. Baker, Rolland. II. Title.

BV3625.M65B34 2007

266.0092′2679—dc22

[B]

2007021718

Contents

Foreword

I cannot think of anyone more qualified to write a book on the subject of expecting miracles than Heidi Baker! As a passionate lover of Jesus, she is His messenger—an apostle of love, a contemporary mystic, a modern-day Mother Teresa.

And *Expecting Miracles* is a book you will not be able to put down. Your life and heart will be challenged to the core as you read the radical adventures of bringing Jesus to cities and nations ravaged by natural disasters, disease, poverty, corruption and circumstances that would make most people run!

Heidi and Rolland's stories will break your heart, shatter your mindsets, uproot deep prejudices and create a longing to do as they do. Their calling crosses a broad expanse as they minister to the poor and dying in Third World nations while being ambassadors of Christ to presidents, dictators, global marketplace entrepreneurs and media. With the true Gospel of the cross and the blood, this book will challenge you to a much deeper and sacrificial walk with Jesus and a strong desire to fulfill the Great Commission.

It is a modern-day book of Acts with adventures that are producing a new breed of lovers who will sacrificially give their lives away, even to the point of martyrdom. Heidi and Rolland teach spiritual truth by sharing visitations. Their radical theology and lifestyle of being laid-down lovers and going through a low door are hallmarks of their lives.

As you read about their amazing exploits, followed by signs and wonders and church growth, your heart will be stirred to love Jesus *and* His people passionately, in a fresh, new way, and you will *never* be the same!

—**Jill Austin**, president and founder
Master Potter Ministries
National and international conference speaker

Chapter 1

Glory from Village to Village

April–May 2005

Update from Rolland Baker

News archive: posted April 8, 2005

Kakala is grinning broadly, so excited. Heidi is prompting her, syllable by syllable, and she is answering perfectly into the microphone. This stirs the whole watching village, which knows that Kakala has been a deaf-mute all her life. They run to get Kakala's mother, and soon the two of them are beaming as they stand together on our revival platform—the flatbed of our three-ton truck. The mother confirms to the whole crowd that she has never heard Kakala speak before.

» p. 18 » p. 18 » p. 19

This is such great news that someone runs off to bring another deaf mute to the meeting—a little girl named Magdalena, much younger than Kakala. Heidi and our ministry team lay hands on her, and instantly she can hear and speak, too. Just minutes ago an older lady got her sight back.

» p. 19 » p. 20

Many have been crowding forward urgently for prayer, and Jesus is gracious. The entire village turned out tonight, and many walked for miles from the countryside when they heard we were coming. They watched the *Jesus* film intently, listened to Heidi preach and testify to the power of God in previous meetings and responded to the Gospel all together with one voice and heart.

This is Heidi's and my third village outreach in the ten days we have been back in Pemba after a long speaking trip. Each time an entire village, without previous exposure to the Gospel, has come to Jesus openly, willingly and eagerly. Each time we pour our hearts out explaining the Gospel as simply, clearly and intensely as we can, and there is no resistance. There in the dark, palm trees silhouetted against a stunningly bright array of Milky Way stars, far from stadiums and big-city lights, the poor in their rags and huts run to Jesus. They receive from Him without hesitation, without doubt. In one night they renounce a lifetime of slavery to witch doctors and evil spirits, false religion and tradition. And they sink to the dirt of their plain village courtyard on their knees to worship the Savior in spirit and truth.

The Moslem province of Cabo Delgado in the far north of Mozambique is receiving the King. In just two years we have seen over 190 churches birthed in villages like this, and every week more are added. The harvest is ripe. This is the time for Mozambique, for all of Africa. The Gospel will burn like fire from the south through North Africa all the way to Jerusalem. May the Body of Christ around the world react to this huge window of opportunity with overcoming faith, limitless love and joyful energy!

While Heidi obediently concentrates on the Makua tribe of Cabo Delgado most of her time, Iris Ministries continues to expand elsewhere. We just had our first conference in Gaza Province in the south, and again everyone listening wanted to partake of the Gospel. Two crippled men who were carried to the meetings left walking on their own. Next week I fly to Medan, Indonesia, following the Holy Spirit in responding to the tsunami victims of Bandah Aceh. Then I fly to the Democratic Republic of the Congo [DR Congo] for more conferences as we pioneer Iris Congo, then Rwanda, Burundi and other countries. . . . We will return to Sudan as we plan outreaches to the north, the south and Darfur in the west. Zimbabwe, Ethiopia and Zambia are calling for help in their great hunger for revival also.

We are building and preparing with all our strength, energy and resources for our school of international ministry this summer, and are expecting some two hundred foreign students, joined by another two hundred national students from Mozambique. May Jesus completely take control of this school and the lives of our students. Anointed speakers are coming from around the world to impart their spiritual understanding and gifts to this body Jesus is bringing together right here on the mission field. In groups, these students will make use of everything they have learned and in the Lord take up the challenge of evangelizing villages in the bush and establishing churches. Jesus, have Your way and make us all fit for Your use just as You desire! Only stay with us, be with us and bring us to life, fired with the glory of Your company and presence!

Nias Island: Onward and upward!

News archive: posted April 23, 2005

» p. 20 » p. 21 » p. 21 » p. 22

Our Merpati Airlines Fokker F-27 is old. The interior is faded and stained. The seats are frayed and tiny. My briefcase won't fit under the seat. But, at least I am on the plane, along with Steve Lazar, director of our children's center at Maputo, and Mel Tari, my evangelist friend of almost thirty years and best man at Heidi's and my wedding. We are headed for Nias Island off the west coast of Sumatra, Indonesia, departing from Medan. But Nias is an earthquake disaster zone, and all flights there are booked up for months. Nobody can get to the island in a hurry without special intervention. And that's just what we get. . . .

Our aging but faithful turboprop airliner is leveling out at only ten thousand feet, allowing a detailed view of the thick Sumatran jungle below. We are near the equator, and all is continually hot and steamy in this part of the world. As I study with wonder the wild, remote, exotic scenery before me, I consider all that God has done to bring the three of us to this point in His even more wondrous unfolding of His purposes in this world. . . .

Twenty-five years ago Heidi and I eagerly took off from Los Angeles International Airport for Indonesia with one-way tickets and thirty dollars in our pockets. We had no support but Jesus, no plan but His voice and no desire but to forsake all and follow Him. Encouraged by the fiery revival in Timor described by Mel in his famous book, *Like a Mighty Wind*, we have pursued the powerful presence of God ever since.

We landed in Bali in the summer of 1980 and over the next few years brought evangelistic dance-drama teams back to Indonesia and all over Asia. Gradually, we learned to slow down and concentrate on the poor. Intent on maintaining Hindu culture in Bali for tourism, Indonesia revoked our missionary visas. We relocated to Hong Kong, very confused and grieved. But we pressed on in the poor back alleys of the glittering big city and made numerous ministry trips to China. Bringing the Good News to "the least of these" became our focus. We took on more and more of the DNA of my grandparents, who saw such an outpouring of the Holy Spirit after taking in wretched beggar children in Kunming, China, where I was born.[1]

The story of our transition to London, England, and then to Africa is told in our book *There Is Always Enough*.[2] For years the Moslem world did not concern us much as we were looking for more fruit than we thought we could expect there. But, through the disastrous floods of 2000 and 2001, revival came to Mozambique. We pressed on, province after province, as desperate villagers in this poorest nation on earth cried out for God. Finally, we came to Cabo Delgado, Mozambique's northernmost province, almost totally Moslem. But, in the last two years we have found that when Moslems see that Jesus is real and that He responds to us with power, beauty and glory when we want Him, they melt in His love. The Gospel is spreading rapidly through "unreachable" Cabo Delgado, and now we, as Iris Ministries, are being led farther up through North Africa as the Holy Spirit prepares the way.

Back to Indonesia

But what of Indonesia, the largest Moslem country in the world, which has seen such revival in some areas and also severe conflict and persecution of Christians? What of our experience there? Nothing is wasted or accidental in our lives as we are formed into His likeness. On December 26, 2004, our attention was suddenly and forcibly drawn back to Asia and to Indonesia in particular. On a flight to Zanzibar in our Cessna, we heard the news of a terrible tsunami that brought unspeakable devastation and grief to the eastern rim of the Indian Ocean.

Shara Pradhan, of Indian descent, was with Heidi and me, and our first response was to send a team immediately to Chennai,

[1] To read about this, see the book *Visions Beyond the Veil* by H. A. Baker, Rolland's grandfather, published by Sovereign World. Available from www.irismin.com and www.sovereignworld.com.

[2] Rolland Baker and Heidi Baker, *There Is Always Enough* (Lancaster, UK: Sovereign World, 2001); North American edition: *Always Enough* (Grand Rapids: Chosen Books, 2004).

India, where some 55,000 people died in the disaster. Many in our Iris family of friends and supporters have been fervently supporting our ministry and relief work there, and we are so encouraged by the power of the Holy Spirit we have seen as a result.

The 9.2 Richter scale earthquake that caused the tsunami set up a wave traveling at 500 miles per hour that landed 65 miles from the epicenter at the beautiful oceanfront town of Banda Aceh on the northern tip of the huge island of Sumatra in Indonesia. Now, months later, we are finding out that probably 300,000 people died along the Aceh coast in a matter of ten minutes, when the energy of the wave hit the land.

There are many Moslems throughout most of Indonesia, but Aceh Province, where the tsunami hit, has been known as the most extreme militant Moslem area of the country. Foreigners were forbidden, and an insurgency had developed against the national government, demanding more independence and Islamic law. Concessions were granted on December 24, and two days later disaster struck. In extreme desperation, Aceh opened up to massive aid from around the world.

Money, personnel and relief goods poured in. Sympathy skyrocketed. Aid management quickly became a massive challenge. Corruption set in. And Christians were almost universally advised to keep a low profile and not take advantage of the situation to advance their faith. Heidi and I wanted Iris to be involved with tsunami relief in Aceh, but with so much aid arriving from secular agencies, we felt our main contribution had to be spiritual. Still, Christian influence from outsiders was not generally welcome, even by other evangelical workers on the scene.

Many Christians did, of course, come to help in any way they could, and Indonesian believers arrived to comfort and pray with the small Banda Aceh church community that survived. I was delayed by my travel schedule for months. But God has His own plan to raise up fiery preachers of the Gospel who will carry His glory with wisdom and power throughout Indonesia, even into the most tragic and resistant of situations.

Two weeks ago a 7.1 aftershock of the tsunami earthquake hit the nearby island of Nias, where I am flying now. Most major buildings were destroyed. Water and power lines were broken. Roads to villages were blocked by cracks and landslides. Businesses were shut down, and many owners fled the island. Food supplies were cut off. The island's infrastructure was crippled, and its 650,000 people were desperate.

Again international aid is pouring in. We land at the airport on this hilly, lush tropical island of palm trees and rich, green foliage and see a familiar sight: cargo planes and helicopters coming and going, aid agency tents set up everywhere, military guards on duty, television crews carrying equipment, boxes of relief goods stacked high. Most volunteers have to find a cot somewhere in the heat and humidity to sleep, but through connections God gave us, we not only got seats on a plane to Nias, but we also find ourselves guests at the governor's house in the main town near the airport.

Driving through town, I begin taking pictures. Street vendors continue to sell what they have right in the rubble and devastation. Children play on piles of collapsed concrete. The few bulldozers on the island begin the massive job of clearing wreckage. We meet the governor, a wonderful Christian man beloved by his people, and he tells of his day-and-night struggle to bring comfort and order to the island. He is sick from breathing dust and fumes, from working around dead bodies and from sheer fatigue. We pray intensely for him.

Life instead of death

The island is 95 percent Christian with over 1,300 church buildings, and we learn that 1,100 of them are completely ruined. The pastors are so discouraged. Few have come to visit and respond spiritually. We suggest a meeting that night of the leading pastors, and it is arranged gladly. Twenty members of the island's pastoral intercessory prayer group gather in the governor's living room under the leadership of Pastor Fatieli Laoli, and Mel, Steve and I begin to minister as the Holy Spirit moves us.

The disasters of life in this world either embitter us against God, leave us numb with no understanding or impress on us just how utterly we need our God—vastly more than we ever felt or realized before. Grief, loneliness and the frailty of life should carry us immediately to the foot of the cross with an overwhelming desire to seek the face of our Savior, until we find in Him what only He can provide. Will the Christians of this island and their leaders, as a result of this cataclysmic event, pursue and carry on with the revival that visited other parts of Indonesia so graciously years ago? Will we rebuild simply and concentrate more on the heart and the Holy Spirit? The Nias church was comfortable, self-contained and in a rut. Can we now hear God's call to come higher, to pursue Him with a passion, to come alive with intensity and be His instruments for righteousness in this nation? Can this disaster turn the many Christians of Nias into a spiritual resource for all of Indonesia?

The pastors cry "Yes!" and they pour their hearts out in prayer. Yes, they want revival; they want miracles and a visitation from God Himself out of the worst Satan can do. They don't want all this pain and suffering to be wasted. They hear and understand. They will exercise all the faith they have and strengthen themselves in the Lord. They will take up the task of testifying to the Gospel of God's grace (see Acts 20:24) in Aceh, the other islands of Indonesia and beyond.

We suggest that churches in America and around the world connect with Nias churches one-on-one to help rebuild them. We would like to start a children's home on Nias and then a Bible school after the pattern we established in Africa, all with the intent of fueling revival and transformation. We would like to invite pastors and short-term missions teams to Nias. We ask the Holy Spirit to control us so that we can participate in God's nature and help fulfill His purposes in this part of the world.

Pastor Laoli's son Berkat fervently tells us of his call to minister to orphans and offers his own house if we will help with expenses. We gladly agree. As a start Berkat will gather thirty children by the end of the week who have fled into the mountains. We will establish Iris Indonesia, set up bank accounts and email, register with the government and put together an Indonesia board of directors, beginning with the governor, Agus Mendrofa.

Back in Medan, we follow through and in a few days are ready to begin. Mel's sister Ice (pronounced "ee-chay") Tari, with 25 years of ministry experience in northern Sumatra, will help lead Iris in Indonesia, along with her friend Lina Gultom, also with a huge heart from Jesus for the poor and suffering. One of the first pastors we are enlisting is a man from Banda Aceh who was in Medan when the tsunami hit, but he lost his wife and all his children. Grief-stricken but unbroken, he has returned to Aceh to minister to his own people. May Jesus Himself be his lover, comfort and joy. Such men will be towers of power and glory in the days to come when a tsunami of the Holy Spirit overwhelms this huge nation. The living God in all His tender mercy and magnificent grandeur knows how to respond to dark despair, and to hearts that cry out to Him alone. Jesus is the Good Shepherd. He will find His lost sheep.

Back in Africa I am about to fly to the Democratic Republic of the Congo in my Cessna for conferences in Goma and Bukavu as we set up Iris Congo there. Heidi is in Brazil. We will both be in Malawi and Mozambique in May at a series of bush conferences. Then in June our missions school begins in Pemba, northern Mozambique, and we will be sending teams out across a whole province. Iris Sudan is getting established step by step under very challenging circumstances, and we are planning outreaches in the Darfur region.

We are extended far beyond any normal, natural capability, but daily we are moved by the beauty of how Jesus works through His Body throughout the world to take care of us and all those He has put under our wings. Our lives in Jesus are miraculous in every detail. We cannot sustain ourselves, but in Him we will not run from disaster. We will be carriers of His glory, always moving forward in faith and not shrinking back. We love and bless you for participating with us in so many ways. May righteousness, peace and joy overtake us together as we enjoy His Presence now and forever!

Why would 15,000 people come to Bangula?

[David Morrison, Iris missionary in Malawi]

Posted May 1, 2005 @ 2:28 P.M.

Report on the bush conference

People come on foot, loaded on flatbed trucks, squeezed into various unroadworthy vehicles. They stream in from near and far. Why? What draws them? They come for food, for the Good News, for fellowship and for healing. Some come because they are curious, some just follow the crowds, hoping for a free meal.

As I work my way through the crowd, people stop me to show me their hungry bellies. I stop to hug a tiny girl whose shoulder blades stand out under her thin dress. At first she is shocked by my touch, and then she draws near. Over and over again my hand is grasped by a little old lady. This year is different. I know some of them; what a gift to recognize friends among the crowds. Careful not to step on sleeping children and their mamas, I continue on my way, praying for God's Spirit to awaken the real hunger, to highlight the deeper need.

As night falls, we worship and dance together. The stage rocks as many feet bang out the rhythms. Heidi preaches. She dances her sermon, every now and then drawing someone in from the crowd. As she speaks about the Father's love for each one of us, she addresses a woman in the crowd: "You, mama, would you feed one of your children and starve the rest?" Everyone laughs. The point is clear. There are no lesser children. Jesus loves each one of us with the same love.

Now I am sitting in the dirt with some of the women. Beside me are a family we came to know through a car accident in December—a boy from a poor village suddenly known and prayed for all over the world, a boy raised to life after three days of unconsciousness—a family wanting to know the life-giver and, consequently, a village with a new church. God's ways are far above our ways!

On my other side some women are dozing. Heidi has also noticed and makes her way across the stage, saying, "Wake up the sleepers, wake them up!" This news is too good to miss. She begins to stretch her hands up and says, "God loves you," and fixing her eyes on one, she draws his attention to the one beside him: "You! Love her." That's how it works. As God's love fills you, you can turn to the one beside you and love him or her. Simple truth, but we cannot skip the first step. Without God's love filling me, I have nothing to offer the hungry child, the desperate grandma or the drunk old man.

Every night there are miracles. The blind see, the deaf hear, the lame walk. The people have no other place to go, and in God's mercy, He hears their desperate cries.

At night, men, women and children stretch out on some poles or on the dirt and sleep. Their bellies are full because today they have eaten; their hearts are full because they have heard the Good News; for many, their sleep is deeper because they are not in pain. They got what they came for. We pray for lasting fruit in their lives.

Update from Rolland Baker photos

1. Heidi with Kakala, a deaf-mute all her life, now healed, hearing and speaking!

2. Kakala speaking to her villager friends with a microphone

3. Kakala with her mother, who had never heard Kakala speak until this night

4. Magdalena, another deaf-mute, healed instantly

5. Heidi with a lady just healed of blindness

Nias Island photos

Severe earthquake damage in the town of Gunungsitoli on Nias Island, Indonesia, resulting from a major aftershock of the earthquake that caused the tsunami of December 26, 2004

CLASS QUALITY

Chapter 2

Fresh Bread

May–June 2005

Congo and beyond!
Somewhere in Central Africa
News archive: posted June 7, 2005

Dark rain clouds loom on the northwest horizon, directly in our flight path. Row after row of mountain ridges stand before us. We have no weather briefing. We have never flown this route before. We are heading for yet another country, but we do not have a landing permit or visas. No airlines fly where we are going, and the journey by road through the forest below is long and dangerous. Air traffic control in Kigali clears us to 8,500 feet on track, releasing us in calm tones to the unknown.

We dodge initial rain flurries, but soon we hit the inevitable downpour. Sheets of water strike our windshield with furious intensity, wildly distorting all forward vision. Our state-of-the-art, noise-canceling headsets barely tame the roar of the rain beating on our Cessna's aluminum skin. But I can see down, and I know from my charts what elevations lie ahead. On we press, our destination less than an hour away.

The storm is very localized, and soon we get through it and move on. But the clouds hang low, and we must descend and angle our way back and forth to clear the wild terrain below by hundreds of feet. Shadowy cliffs and peaks materialize and fade in the mist. Huts hide in tiny clearings among trees on hilltops. Now the ridges are lower, and ahead we get our first sight of the lake we are expecting. We see only a corner of it, but we are excited because we know it marks the border of our next ministry frontier, the Democratic Republic of the Congo!

Soon Lake Kivu opens up before us, a jewel sixty miles long with its inlets and islands spread below in a creative array almost five thousand feet high in the very center of Africa. We are far from the plains of the Serengeti that we flew over yesterday and even farther from the beaches and sand of Mozambique more than a thousand miles behind us. We are compelled to preach the Gospel here, too. In the service of our King, we have eagerly taken hold of this opportunity to bring more revival fire to a region long isolated by instability, violence and bloodshed.

» p. 33 » p. 33 » p. 34

Obviously, a small private plane hasn't landed here in years. Soldiers in combat fatigues, carrying machine guns and rocket launchers, stand nearby and stare at us with near disbelief. Officials and military officers press forward, soon hammering us with questions: "Where is your permit?" "Who said you could land here?" "What are you doing here?"

That's why we have Joseph with us. He has made informal verbal agreements with airport officials at Goma for our entry into the Congo—our one option at the time—but Goma has no aviation gas, and we only had enough fuel to fly straight to Bukavu and back. Before this flight Joseph assured us that landing directly at Bukavu, his hometown, would be no problem, but now we have a very big problem. We are drawn into an office, just an empty room with a bare desk, for a major, lengthy "discussion." Joseph is masterfully calm, and Surpresa [one of our international directors] and I just stay quiet. It emerges that Joseph is known as a local church leader and is respected by all involved. Phone calls are made, voices are lowered, papers are signed and we are given stern instructions for the future. God has prepared the way in exceptional circumstances through the favor of a godly reputation.

Armed guards let us out of the gate, and another crowd is waiting for us—this time laughing, shouting, jumping and waving their arms with excitement. They are local Christians, and they are overjoyed. The Iris missionaries have come! They are not alone. Jesus has heard their prayers. Their family in God is growing. Let revival burn! The people have been waiting for days. Many have come long distances. Everyone is expectant; the mood is electric. This is a tremendous moment! Jesus has not forgotten them. Let's have church.

We gradually move to the conference "center."

Bukavu conference

Mud and water are all over the floor under scattered benches. There's a tin roof, but it's not big enough and we have to put up plastic sheeting for the rain. There's no electricity, but we brought a generator, and soon I have our sound system set up. Hundreds of people are crowded in, and we can begin our first session.

» p. 34 » p. 35 » p. 35 » p. 36

We realize we are in a different sort of place. This is not church as usual. The people will not be denied. They cannot passively wait on God. In their extremity they know Jesus is their only hope. They can do only one thing: cry out with every ounce of life remaining in their souls. Existence in this world has been so cruel to these people that they don't look for relief anywhere but the Creator and Redeemer Himself. Without any effort on our part, Surpresa and I watch the Holy Spirit release these hearts passionately reaching out for life.

The Holy Spirit continues to fall strongly on us for three days. Some, of course, are watching wide-eyed and wondering from the back, but in the front, desire and faith are igniting a real revival. The Holy Spirit is emotional and passionate and often very physical. He is intense, burning up with love, anxious to break out and overcome people with supernatural life. He knows how to respond to each person's cries and how each needs to be loved. The blazing presence of God burns out every evil thought, each petty desire, all selfish ambition. There is nothing left but what God wants, what He values, what dazzles and thrills Him! We are being transformed into fit companions for the King!

As always during these frontline forays into new territory, it is an extreme challenge to present in our limited time what the people most need to hear. But increasingly we learn to relax and flow with the Holy Spirit, praying that God's every purpose for this trip will be fulfilled. Through all the tears and laughter, repentance and joy, worship and celebration, healings and deliverances, we find time to teach the most basic and critical foundations of the Gospel. This movement does not chase health and wealth or manifestations or signs and wonders. We preach Jesus and Him crucified and the power of the cross. Nothing counts but faith working through love, producing joy! We seek first His kingdom and His righteousness, and all these other things will chase us! We are learning how to be rich in good deeds and blessed with godliness and contentment. We are falling in love with Him who is love, until nothing in this world attracts us like He does. . . .

June blog entry from Meredith and Monica
[two students in Iris Missions School]
Posted June 27, 2005 @ 7:40 P.M.

Here are some thoughts we've been wrestling with. We decided to write from our journals, for it is hard to know where to begin to describe this experience. Hopefully, it's not too heavy, and it's not meant to discourage those of us who do have wealth. This is just the transparency of our thoughts. When all is said and done, God is sovereign and just and abounding in love. . . .

They stood up one by one. Upon their faces rested a countenance of fullness. Fullness of the Spirit. Through their eyes blazed a sense of strength birthed from great pain. Lemos, one of the pastors we have befriended, stood among the children of God who knew suffering to a depth we cannot fathom. Each one of the pastors stood because someone in their immediate family has died from starvation: a mother . . . a child . . . a wife.

Lemos is a man who bears much fruit of joy, patience and humility. Never is he at a loss for a beautiful smile as he exclaims, "*Gracias Deus*" ("Praise God"). He has lived and survived in the midst of great hunger and death. We suppose that one would imagine death would produce the fruit of bitterness and resentment—especially toward our Creator. Yet, every day we have seen him [Lemos], he is filled with the joy of the Lord.

> "Blessed are those who hunger and thirst for righteousness,
> for they will be filled."
>
> Matthew 5:6

Our teacher spoke this afternoon about hungering after righteousness, the Kingdom of God. She commented on how differently these Mozambican pastors look at the Scriptures, because the word *hunger* has a whole other meaning to them. They know that hunger unfulfilled leads to death. These pastors have experienced that hunger. They have a desperation for this righteousness with the same yearning that they have for food. These men and women view the whole Gospel in a different light than we do in the West—the words of Jesus take on a different meaning and depth in the eyes of the poor.

The pastors then came and laid hands upon us to pray that we would experience a deep hunger for the Spirit of God. When they prayed, we did not understand all the words, but we could hear the desperation in their voices. We wept. We stood there as the rain poured forth from our souls onto the dry desert of apathy and complacency that cripples us from truly seeking God. Language, culture, skin color, gender, class—all of these are illusory boundaries within the human race. But the Spirit of God can unify any people group who truly call on His name. These Mozambican pastors, though poor in material wealth, possess a wealth we long to draw from and a heart we are constantly learning from.

Last night it was Mozambique's Independence Day. A restaurant was serving a traditional meal to celebrate. Of course, only the rich were invited. How strange, how uncomfortable, how it truly wrenches the soul to be in a country where the wealth we possess is unfathomable to the people here. We sat and ate a grand feast at the oceanside as little children peeked through the walls of palm leaves to behold foods they would probably never be able to afford. An eerie feeling accompanies the knowledge that we are a group of people in this world who are blessed with material possessions and knowing we have our next meal on the table.

With the knowledge of this blessing comes the question of our responsibility to those who do not have assurance of their next meal. Can we truly abide in Christ and not carry a burden to address the issue of poverty? For right now we're contemplating that to ignore the existing disparity between the wealth and poverty is to break ourselves from the heart of God. How easily we could live life, ignoring the existing injustices of the world. And these thoughts push us far beyond our comfort zone as we contemplate how such thoughts will manifest into action. Where can we go from here?

We left the restaurant with a stomach full of gourmet foods and spirits full of bewilderment. Not guilt, but bewilderment over how we could sit and eat such a feast when there were poor people dying of famine. How does such a disparity exist? We've learned guilt and shame are not fruits of the Spirit, so we are continually asking God to spare us from guilt and fill our souls with abounding love and joy. Guilt seems to keep us from being able to love anybody. It is not guilt that we are carrying, but a question of how God desires for us to live in the world of "haves" and "have-nots." It is a question we wrestle with daily.

Upon returning to the children's center, there was a sight to behold. The pastors were running out of the worship area in a state of great joy and excitement, each carrying a blue plastic bag of new things. Honestly, we haven't sensed such excitement in the center since we have been here. Each of their faces carried such light, like a child on Christmas morning. In the bag was a brand-new shirt, a toothbrush, toothpaste, a pen and soap. They immediately put on their new shirts, replacing the old shirts with holes and rips. Because they have so little, there was such an abundance of joy upon receiving the gift. There was a huge celebration among the pastors that night, and it carried over into the next morning. Our friend was wearing his brand-new blue shirt as he looked at us with such excitement, explaining that someone in America bought the shirt for him. Truly, it is better to give than to receive.

To walk in upon this, after our feast at the restaurant that we barely appreciated, overwhelmed us. We just sat at the base of the huge baobab tree and looked up at the full moon in a state of bewilderment. All we could hear in our spirits was, *This is reality.* There will always be wealth and poverty, famine, war and disease. All these things are going to increase while a select few live in a surreal mirage of abundance. All we can do is choose how to live our lives. Our prayer is to learn how to love God and our neighbors as ourselves in the midst of such extremities.

Responses to blog posting

Tom Cooper: September 28, 2005 @ 11:46 A.M.

Having made *aliyah* [immigration] from the United States to Israel, I have learned much about the blinding wealth of Western culture, and yet, as difficult as life here can be, I still have an abundance of good things that the people of Mozambique will likely never have this side of heaven.

I have often been struck with this same bewilderment and have fought off the pangs of guilt, knowing that God decides who we are and where we shall be born, whether into wealth or poverty. As you said, it is up to us what kind of lives we live—what we do with that wealth or how we respond in our poverty. The apostle Paul said he had learned to be content in either. I believe his contentment was a result of his obedience to the Holy Spirit.

I pray the Lord will give me and my family right perspectives, heavenly values and hearts of selfless giving in order that we may be the servants rather than the served.

Neal: September 28, 2005 @ 8:52 P.M.

The past few days I have been asking God why people don't always get baptized in the Holy Spirit when they ask. And how come we don't see many healings? Why do we pray for the addict and not see him or her delivered? After reading this blog and your remarks, it is all too clear: "Hunger after righteousness," and we will see these things happening.

Life principles: Fresh bread

More than the food and drink we need to live, we need fresh bread from heaven. We need the bread of life that only Jesus can provide—His glorious presence. Those who are spiritually hungry will be satisfied as they eat and drink of Jesus. My prayer is constantly that God would give us such a hunger for Him, and that He would pour out the healing oil of His Holy Spirit on all who are desperate for Him. We need to welcome such hunger. We need to be like helpless little children before our Savior, giving Him full and absolute control of every area of our lives. Then we will know that, truly, Jesus is more than enough.

Several years ago, the Lord gave me a vision that is mentioned in our first book, *There Is Always Enough*, but I will mention it briefly here. Ever since this day I have been wrecked and ruined by His love. I saw thousands and thousands of hungry children, all begging to be fed. I knew I had the responsibility of feeding them, and it totally overwhelmed me. I remember screaming out in panic and desperation, shouting, "No, no, no! There are too many!" There was such a multitude of children pressing toward me that it seemed impossible that they could ever be fed by one person. I couldn't understand how on earth it was possible. At that time we cared for around 320 children, and I thought that was a lot.

But then Jesus showed me His face, and that changed everything for me. He gazed at me with eyes of love that pierced my soul. He looked right into me with eyes that were like liquid oil and fire at the same time. He melted my heart. His face was so indescribably glorious, shining and bright, yet I noticed that His body was broken—broken by the suffering He endured for us. And then He said to me, *Take this.* He reached into His side and took a small piece of His own body and placed it into my hand. Right in my hand it turned into bread. Jesus said to me, *Now, give it to them to eat.* I began to pass out the bread and every child ate—all those thousands and thousands of hungry mouths. Then Jesus said to me, *I died so that there would always be enough.*

We don't comprehend how much of God's presence is available to us. Jesus so wants to fill us with His Spirit that there will always be *more than enough*. Not for us to selfishly consume ourselves, but to give away! Jesus wants to fill us to overflowing so that His presence will touch every single person who crosses our path in life.

Often, we are so spiritually malnourished that we have nothing to offer anyone. We are weak vessels because we spend all our resources chasing after that which is not satisfying. But we need the presence of God more than we need anything else in life. It is only His presence that will truly satisfy us. God is looking for people who are hungry enough for Him alone that they will be able to feed a nation with His presence.

Anyone who is desperate enough for Jesus will be satisfied! Thank God there is nothing in ourselves that we can do to earn this provision—it has been paid for already! But we need a hungry heart to receive. And when we do, Jesus multiplies whatever He pours into us until we find ourselves feeding others—the spiritually desperate and starving. He wants to place something of Himself in our hands that will be a provision to many.

We live in a broken world. Jesus wants us to notice and help those around us who are so in need of His presence. He wants us to reach out to them. But we can't go to them empty-handed. We need the fresh bread of His presence to feed the starving.

Congo and beyond photos

1. Flying over Lake Kivu

2. Bukavu's beautiful setting

3. Lake Kivu

Bukavu conference photos

1. Our church conference parking lot entrance

2. Children of Bukavu at the church door

3. Cooking for the conference

4. We baptized many who came to Jesus at the lakeside in Bukavu

Chapter 3

Hungry for Jesus

June–July 2005

Rolland's June 2005 update

Our pace continues to accelerate. In May we hosted hundreds of visitors who came to participate in major conferences in the bush of Mozambique and Malawi—a tremendous logistical challenge. Thirty thousand gathered in the remote town of Morrumbala, Surpresa's birthplace, for meetings with Todd Bentley and his Fresh Fire team, and twenty thousand in Bangula, Malawi, with Ché Ahn and his HIM [Harvest International Ministry] team. We and our staff threw ourselves into the ministry with all our hearts and strength as well, seeing God do many miracles among us all. We have so much more to report!

Next, our staff journeyed to Bilene far to the south for our annual staff retreat, a richly appreciated and needed time when our own Iris family could relax and enjoy the powerful presence of God. Heidi, Surpresa and I loved this chance to bless and encourage our "troops" and for us all to be greatly stirred by our prophetic guest speaker, Jill Austin.

Then Todd, Ché, their teams and the rest of us headed for our northern base of Pemba and continued meetings there in a large tent we just shipped in from Dubai. At the same time, our new school of missions geared up with more than two hundred international students. Pemba's remoteness and limited infrastructure resulted in construction delays and other stressful conditions that exposed visitors dramatically to the reality of how most of the world lives. But beautiful and willing hearts plunged in and helped on all sides, and the Holy Spirit is richly on the school. Many have come to be utterly broken, transformed and taken to a new level, and they will get the desire of their hearts.

» p. 50

And so the Holy Spirit is moving among us and other ministries around the world faster than we ever imagined. We have lost our love of this world. The Kingdom is our pearl of great price. Our King is our greatest possession. And the poor and desperate of the world are running to Him. They will not miss His fire and glory. They will not be left behind. They will not lose the riches of their inheritance in Him.

Jesus is worth something. He is worth everything! We ask our readers, "Who will lose their lives for Him in order to gain them? Who will suffer hardship as good soldiers of Jesus Christ and run the race to win? Who will join us in the harvest field, sparing nothing? Who wants to burn with life and passion in pursuit of what is pure, perfect and eternal? Who wants to love as Jesus loves?"

Heidi's blog entry

July 3, 2005 @ 1:00 A.M.

I so need you to pray for me. I am longing for more of Jesus. These last two weeks we have been in many intense storms. I know Jesus is in the boat and He calms the storm. The amazing thing is how He has come in supernatural power in a way I have seldom seen. We have combined the Bible college and missions school every afternoon in Pemba, Cabo Delgado. In His lovely grace, the Holy

Spirit has been falling upon the four hundred students day after day. I love seeing people from all over the world, worshiping with new Mozambican believers. I love seeing piles of people weeping on grass mats in the dirt as Jesus pours His glory love out on the people. I loved baptizing 43 new believers in the sparkling turquoise waters of Pemba this Sunday afternoon. I preached about full immersion in the glory heart of Jesus' love. The Lord is calling us deeper into the river of His love. He is asking us to come to the lowest place of love and allow the river of God to come over our heads. He leads us to a place where we are so covered in His love no one sees us anymore. We have the mind of Christ and stay in the low place of love.

Outreach this week was in a nearby village. I preached a salvation message in this unreached area, and nearly everyone wanted to receive Jesus as Lord and Savior. I felt God ask me to challenge the people to bring the blind, deaf and crippled to be healed.

» p. 50

I held a deaf and mute man in my arms and prayed for him to hear and speak in the name of Jesus. His tongue was immediately loosed, and his ears opened up. For the first time in fifteen years, he spoke and heard! It was beyond beautiful.

The next lady had not heard anything in twelve years. I put my fingers in her ears and commanded her ears to be opened in the name of Jesus. Her smile lit up my world as Jesus opened her deaf ears.

Next, some missions students brought me a little boy around twelve years of age. He had been completely blind since birth and was sent away from his village by his parents to beg in the city. His guide who led him around the streets of Pemba was with me on the truck. I spit on my fingers and put them on his eyelids. I held him in my arms and rocked him back and forth as I felt the deep love the Father had for this boy. When I asked Jesus to open his eyes, he saw light for the first time! He looked around in amazement as his eyes were opened by the glorious love and grace of Jesus. I held him close and began to weep at the beauty of what Jesus had just done.

After such a fabulous miracle, others pressed forward to receive their healing. A lady with a crippled foot for ten years leaped for joy as her foot was made whole by the Lamb of God. Drunks came weeping to the front, declaring their desire to be saved.

No matter what we go through, we will get through because we are in love with the One who is altogether lovely. He continues to call us to care for the orphans and widows. We took in many more this week. One little boy was transfixed in the presence of God with tiny hands lifted to his God. In the end, the heavy, weighty glory of God fell upon this child who had just met Jesus.

I am truly undone by the love of Jesus. Please keep praying for us. Please don't forget us or our thousands of children. You are loved.

Heidi

Responses to blog posting

Nikki: July 31, 2005 @ 12:50 A.M.

I wept longingly as I read your letter. I am 28 and have been a Christian for 24 years. After all these years my eyes are being opened by the overwhelming love of Jesus! Compassion for the lost, hurt and dying has gripped my heart in such a way that I have never experienced before.

Deanna S: July 31, 2005 @ 8:54 A.M.

Every time I read what is going on, I want to be there. I pray earnestly for the [people of the] Western world to humble themselves and pray that we, too, will see the love and glory of the Father as Africa is seeing right now. Not just here and there, but all the time. I weep each time I read what God is doing for the lost—so much love. I am so undone by His love.

Heather H: August 1, 2005 @ 5:43 A.M.

Thank you for the amazing testimonies of Jesus' love and power. They make my spirit leap with joy! Thank you for continuing to lay your life down and for sharing with us your hunger for more of Jesus. It is contagious! The testimonies that you share fuel the fire within me to want so much more of Him as well.

Rolland's blog entry

July 8, 2005 @ 2:31 A.M.

Hi, our wonderful friends in the Body of Christ! Your entries in this blog are so extremely encouraging, and Heidi and I feel very loved by Jesus through you! I will try to add reports and comments as I travel in remote locations so you don't have to wait for newsletters to hear from us. May Jesus be honored and glorified here, and may many be encouraged to run the race to win. Please keep writing!

Responses to blog posting

David S: July 10, 2005 @ 11:45 P.M.

It is a great encouragement for me to hear how God is advancing His Kingdom in Africa and how He can work when there is faith. What encourages me the most is seeing how God is working through your weakness, not your strength. He is so amazingly powerful.

Pippa S: July 16, 2005 @ 12:20 A.M.

I struggle so much with the apathy and cynicism over here in the West. We have so much that we Christians tend to no longer depend on the Lord. In other words, we have gotten too comfortable. Your book has helped me fall more deeply in love with my Savior. I have just finished university, and it is my long-term desire to work and live in Africa.

Interview with Pastor Maparo Matola

[A brief interview with one of Iris's indigenous pastors]

My name is Maparo Matola. I am now 26 years old. I am pastoring a church in Patrus, Momoomba, in one of the suburbs in Maputo. I have been with Iris Ministries for two years.

How did you become a Christian?

I grew up in a Christian family, reading my Bible. At one point I thought there was no need for me to get saved. Then one day I was listening to Mama Ida [Heidi] preaching. She said, "Those who want to go to heaven right now, they've got to receive Jesus." So I went up and received Jesus. From that point on I started learning, learning, learning about the things of God! But, soon after that, I got a job and stayed away from the church. I was more devoted to my work than serving God. But after a year, the Lord spoke to me and called me into full-time ministry. So I spoke to Mama Ida and she gave me some advice. She wanted to know if I wanted to be in a Bible school for two years. That's how I started in ministry.

Why do you think miracles happen now?

I believe God loves, with people who do not believe, to show that He is the power to heal. For our part, we just have to have faith. God wants to show that by faith, people can get healed.

Since I have been sent out from Iris, I have seen God do a lot of things, especially miracles. I used to pray for a lot of people, expecting them to get healed, but those things were not happening. But I kept on praying and praying and praying and praying. In these last days, I have seen God do many miracles. At times I pray for someone who is sick, and instantly that person gets healed. At times we have been singing a song in praise and worship, and a person will just get up and give a testimony and say, "When I came here I was sick, but during the worship just now I am feeling well."

Recently, I prayed for the first time for a person who was deaf. Since he was born, he didn't have any hearing or speech. So he came to the church and we prayed. Instantly he was healed! So we have seen a lot of things, especially miracles.

How many people are in your church?

Now we have 350 people. We have a lot of home cell groups. If the people grow their group to around twenty, we plant a church. Each day during the week, we go and visit all the cell groups, day after day. But on Sunday we all come together, all of us.

How many people are coming to Christ—becoming Christians each week?

We don't have people coming to Christ every week—they come to Christ every day! Every day we have ten to twenty people come to Christ. During the day we go to the markets, the bus stations, the schools, the hospitals, and talk about Jesus, and every day people want to come to Him.

What do you think is going to happen in the future for your church?

I have a great expectation that there will be a real moving of the Holy Spirit. In the past years, people have not really believed in the Holy Spirit. They have thought that the Holy Spirit was just for the Pentecostal churches or for the white people. But what I am seeing and what I am experiencing is that the fire of the Holy Spirit is really moving in Mozambique.

Mozambique news

Monica Miller: late June/early July 2005

You know you're in Pemba, Mozambique, when . . .

1. You're standing quietly in a crowd, minding your own business, when a baby on the back of the woman in front of you pees on your foot.
2. A monkey on a string bites you on the way to church.
3. You have to carry your Bible to the altar call because someone might steal it.
4. Your skin lightens a whole shade after a shower.
5. *Dressing up* means wearing clothes that have been worn only once, and *freshening up to go out* consists of using a baby wipe.
6. Like a mad woman, you run around the back of the church during the altar call because you itch so badly.
7. You jump up and down for joy because you just got a lightbulb for the bathroom.
8. Living with twelve girls in one room is considered "getting space" (because you lived with thirty girls previously).
9. You are so moved by the Spirit that you have to go jump into the ocean, only to end up sitting on a rock, crying as a strange fisherman picks a sea urchin out of your foot.
10. The bathroom is a hole in the ground.
11. Goat for dinner sounds really good.

As you can tell, life here is as amusing as it is perplexing. We are happy, healthy and slightly dirty.

Seloma ["hello" in native Makua], my beautiful family and friends. I continue to stand in awe at how God is moving here in Africa and wanted to give you a brief update.

Recently, God has been using me to connect with the women and children in the community. Every week I take different orphans for ice cream or to the beach, to swim, to play—just to give them a special break and one-on-one attention.

I have developed friendships with several women my age in the village of Pemba and try to spend time with them each week. Great news in Pemba—they have just started a church! This new church has been in existence for only three Sundays and is wonderful—lots of singing and dancing. Every Sunday it gets bigger. It is a large tent (like a circus tent), and I would estimate two hundred villagers attended this Sunday. Fifty people came to the altar to become Christians. The small wood-plank altar almost broke from the weight of those praying. Glory!

As many of you remember, I felt particularly led that some of the donations you provided should fund Portuguese Bibles for the new African ministers being trained by Iris Ministries. Well, let me tell you about this! In late June, 178 newly trained pastors received their Bibles as part of their commissioning service. Along with the Bibles, they also received a pen and a notebook. I cannot express how profoundly meaningful these gifts are to them. Other than the clothes on their backs, these are typically their only possessions. As soon as they could, they began writing their names all over their Bibles to make them their own treasured possessions.

Although most of the pastors are male, there are five female pastors. This makes me happy, and I have poured time on them, getting to know them and learning from them. I am so in awe of them! In addition to being ministers, they are also doing the many things African women do every day, such as being the gatherers of food, cooking food and taking care of the children. Many African women are like single parents, since the men go to urban areas to look for work. It is a difficult life. But it has been wonderful to discover that African women are not looked down on here; it is more common to see female leaders.

How has Africa increased my faith? Where do I start? I see healing as I have never experienced in my life. This is where the Gospel in Africa is ten times better than in the West! They are super desperate for the Word of God. They believe and they get healed. The simplicity of their faith is powerful! They are so hungry. If you can imagine the most starving person, the Africans are ten times more starving for God—so hungry and thirsty for the Word! How they read and understand the Gospel in Africa is powerful. I have never seen this kind of believing in God. When you look at the Scriptures through the eyes of Africans, they instantly grasp "Seek ye first the kingdom and all things will be added." They believe with everything in them! You see famine disappear; you see villages being healed and professing Jesus.

I am learning about what gifts I have and how to pray and let things happen, to let God work through me. God has used me to be a blessing of healing. I lay my hands on many people and pray for their healing. Some are considered "untouchable." Every person I have prayed for has had something happen, some healing in his or her life. Not an instant healing, but later, days later, they seek me out to share how they have been healed or changed. The power of love is so huge! Touching the lowest and loving on them—nothing is more powerful than that.

Dealing with the contrast of my life and the poverty of Africans has been the hardest part of my work. I go through feeling guilty about having so much wealth. I am so blessed to have something as basic as hot and cold water at home. When I see villagers in Pemba licking water from puddles, I weep. I often weep at the many injustices, and when I weep, I pray and read the Scriptures. The Word has given me much comfort, especially the Old Testament prophets. There is always hope in the prophets, particularly in Isaiah. Yes, God has given me an eye to see injustice, but through His Word I find the assurance that ultimately love and joy will surpass the injustice. This is the blessing.

I am learning how to get back to the Father's heart. It is like the true nature of God. I feel so much incarnate love through the African pastors. I love what they teach me through their eyes. I have so much more love and joy just in being here. I am made to be here; I am made to be in Africa and live with the poor. I feel such a sense of peace, love and joy that is very real and wonderful!

Agape,
Monica Miller
Student, Holy Given missions school, Pemba, Mozambique

Life principles: The hungry always get fed

Are you hungry?

Something we have learned by feeding the poor is that the hungry always get fed. The hungry eat; the thirsty drink. They are radical about their hunger. They are so concerned with being fed that they dispense with all apathy. There is no "Well, if we get it, we get it; if we don't, we don't. . . . "

Sometimes the Church is like that. "Whatever God wants to do is okay with me," we say. "I'm here if He wants to show up." Yet there is something about the person with an all-consuming desperation for Jesus that touches His heart.

I freely admit that I am a glutton for God. I am so desperate for whatever God has to offer me that I will let people from any stream of church life pray for me. It makes no difference to me who they are, where they are from or what they look like. If they have an anointing from God, then I want it, too!

Once, a minister prayed for me and God really touched me. Our backgrounds and experiences were so different it made my head spin. I had been living in the slums for years, working with the poor, walking in the dirt. My friend wore an $8,000 suit and spoke about the $15 million house he owned. To say that the worlds we lived in were a little different would be a gross understatement.

But he had an anointing. So I didn't give a rip about his $15 million house. I thought, *Whatever that guy has, I'm getting it.* I did this because I am a glutton for God. I didn't want his house, but I did want his anointing. I didn't care about the package. The package can upset you. But who cares about the package? We must go for whatever God has for us, because we know it will always be good.

I spend a lot of time at the garbage dump. It is my favorite place to be. The people there are so hungry that when it comes time to eat, they literally stomp on each other. They are so desperate that they push and shove each other out of the way in order to get to the food first. It does not sound nice, I know, but the ones who scream the loudest and push the hardest get fed first. The ones who press in always get the bread.

I have witnessed this happen time and again, so I asked God, "What is this, God?" He said, *The ones who are hungry get fed. The ones who are thirsty get to drink.* It is as simple as that.

Spiritually speaking, most believers in the West live on junk food: cotton candy, Diet Coke, Twinkies. This is all they ever eat, yet they complain they are tired. Why are they tired? Because they are trying to live on junk food! Why do people try to survive on junk when God has laid out a feast for us to eat? Instead of consuming stuff that makes us sick, we need to eat that which will make us strong and well. We need constantly to eat of Jesus. We need to drink of Him.

My prayer for you is that God may provoke you to a holy hunger.

Isaiah 55:1 says,

> "Come, all you who are thirsty,
>   come to the waters;
> and you who have no money . . ."

Sometimes the Western Church feels disqualified by its wealth. In Africa it is impossible to feel that way because of the poverty.

When it is time for church in Africa, we never have any parking problems when the people turn up. If we have even one car in the parking lot when four thousand people gather to worship, it is a big deal: "Wow! Who has a car? It must be somebody really important."

In Africa we cannot come to God any other way than with our poverty. But in the West we often have the mentality that we must pay for the free gifts God wants to give us. The greatest trap is thinking we have to pay for God's blessings with our spiritual discipline. I teach on spiritual discipline all the time, but here is a fact: You cannot pay someone for food that has already been given freely. You cannot pay for something that has already been purchased by the blood of the Lamb. It is free!

If you are thirsty, God invites you to come and drink. He wants you to come without your money. Leave your wallet at home, because you cannot buy this food and drink. It is not for sale.

> "Why spend money on what is not bread,
> and your labor on what does not satisfy?
> Listen, listen to me, and eat what is good,
> and your soul will delight in the richest of fare."
>
> Isaiah 55:2

Don't waste your time consuming what makes you weak. Spend your time pressing in for the Presence. Become so intimate with Jesus, so full of Him, that it does not matter what challenges in life present themselves to you. You will be so spiritually full that you can feed a multitude of other people's needs. Jesus will give you more than enough!

Rolland's June 2005 update photo

Heidi speaking to a visiting team at Pemba

Heidi's blog entry photo

Baptisms on the beach in Pemba

Chapter 4

Christ of the Rubbish Dump

July–August 2005

Rolland's blog entry for July

Posted July 8, 2005 @ 2:31 A.M.

Hi, our wonderful friends in the Body of Christ! Your entries in this blog are so extremely encouraging, and Heidi and I feel very loved by Jesus through you! I will try to add reports and comments as I travel in remote locations so you don't have to wait for newsletters to hear from us. May Jesus be honored and glorified here, and may many be encouraged to run the race to win. Please keep writing!

Much, much love in Him,
Rolland

Reponse to blog posting

Heather Harmon: July 13, 2005 @ 5:34 A.M.

Thank you both not only for pouring your lives into Africa, but also for pouring yourselves into the Western Church. In the past few years I have come to know a Jesus that the Church never taught me about. I finally get it—it is all about climbing the mountain of sacrifice to the lowest place I've ever been, so I can lay down to love the One who loves to be loved and is the Lover of my soul. It is about continually going to the secret place, going deeper and deeper to the point of total immersion. It is here that not only are the strategies of heaven revealed, but also where I gain complete understanding of the fact that I am not an orphan, but rather an adopted child of the King! However, I must not stop here! Now I can run, unafraid, into the darkest places of the world as a laid-down lover and a shining light of Jesus Christ, continuing to carry the joy (because God is always in a good mood!) and learning to love because it's all about LOVE.

Perspectives of Iris Ministries pastors

[The following was posted on the blog site by David Barker, a visiting pastor from Australia, who interviewed a number of Iris pastors and who also recalls his own memories of the visit.]

[Talking to Pastor John]

Witch doctors converted

I have been a minister for eight years now. I am in the Shopa Province, Gaza, Mozambique. I have been in the Gaza Province for four years. I thank God that He is really using me in this area. I have already planted fourteen cell churches. [Note: When a cell gets up to twenty members, they split and form another cell and continue growing.] I am 27 years old.

God is really using me in healing right now. I have prayed for so many people with different sicknesses and diseases, even for people who have demons. Recently, I prayed for a person who was very sick and was in a bed for six months, unable to do anything. We went to his area to do a crusade. I went to his house, I prayed for him and he was instantly healed. So, he got out of his bed and came to the crusade! His family was really ecstatic.

We have also seen the witch doctors coming to Jesus. Currently, in my church I have six former witch doctors who have been saved. When they were saved they burned everything they had used when they were witch doctors. These people have been discipled for several years and are now very strong in the Lord. God is using them to heal other people. They want more from God. And now, they are having the opportunity to train the young people in the ways of God.

[Talking to Trainee Pastor Ivan. Ivan was among the first children living in the Iris orphanage when it was first established by Heidi and Rolland in 1995. He is now 21 years old, shines with the love of Christ and is training as a lay pastor in the Bible school.]

Bread miracle for the poor

Every week we are helping the poor here in street outreach ministry. Once, a few years ago, we went out to buy bread down the street. We bought fifty loaves of bread and we distributed it to the poor people in the street, and the bread was not enough. We did not have enough money in our pockets to buy more bread. So what we did was to look to Jesus and pray and put the bread in the middle of us. Then we prayed a second time. When we looked up, some total strangers had come along with some more boxes of bread and gave the bread to us right then and there. These people bringing the bread did not know Jesus, they just felt compelled at that time to come along with some bread for the poor and suffering.

We are so happy because we know that God is touching people. God is still working deeply in Mozambique. And we know that Jesus is for us. If we believe, then Jesus shows He is the Bread of Life for us!

Christ of the rubbish dump

David Barker: posted July 22, 2005 @ 8:37 A.M.

While visiting the Iris Ministries Orphanage in Maputo, Mozambique, I had an opportunity to go to a church service at the *bocaria* [the massive rubbish dump outside Maputo]. Fellow visitors Mark and Sue, along with Katrina (a German missionary), our local Mozambican translator, Dominguez (a student from the Bible school), and I met at the vehicle compound and prayed for the meeting and that our vehicle would not be ransacked while we were inside the church! Katrina suggested that anyone who received a word from the Lord during the worship should be prepared to share it. We climbed into the truck and drove for ten minutes from the orphanage to the rubbish dump. Dominguez could understand English better than he could speak it and was anxious that he would do it justice, so as we drove along, Mark led us in praying for him.

We arrived at the rubbish dump as night set in, drove down a bumpy dirt lane to the side of the tip, then turned right. Towering off and up to our right were hundred-meter-high piles of rubbish, stretching out for a kilometer back up the hill to the main road. Every fifty meters or so, there were fires burning as a means of reducing the volume of waste. Smoke wafted overhead, the stench a combination of the fires and the refuse. There were silhouettes of men rummaging here and there, looking for food or resellable scraps. The scene was apocalyptic.

Heidi had first begun to visit the dump regularly in the early years of their [her and Rolland's] ministry in the mid-'90s, as they knew this is where the down-and-outs of society in Third World countries congregate. They began to take street kids off the dump and into their Iris center. Eventually they began outreach meetings, and soon a church was formed. A small plot of land was purchased at the bottom of the dump, and a church building (dirt floor, thatched walls and thatched roof) was established.

We could hear the singing immediately as we parked the car outside the front of the church. We walked into a dimly lit room. Two kerosene lanterns hung from the supporting branch poles. A narrow five-foot concrete platform formed the front of the room. On the platform were seven kids ranging from a couple of sixteen-year-old girls down to five-year-olds, and they were leading the worship. All you could see of their faces were their smiles, it was so dark! They sang passionately, nasally and in tune. In front of them on the dirt floor was the local pastor. Facing them was the congregation, 25 all told, and some kids dressed in thin cotton clothes. The singing finished, and the pastor began to pray. He poured his heart out in a desperate prayer, his voice rising and falling with the anguish and desire in his heart. He pleaded with the Lord for fifteen minutes in the local Shangi dialect [one of seven main languages and 48 dialects in Mozambique].

Mark, a qualified minister, walked over to Katrina and said he had received a word during the worship. Katrina got up, introduced the visitors, then invited Mark to share. Mark shared a good word about drawing closer to God in intimate, passionate worship. He said that the people would be given new songs to sing, taking them into a deeper intimacy with Jesus. Then he prayed an impartational prayer over everyone while the worship singers sang. It was holy chaos for a while as Mark shouted above the singing, along with the translator. He then began laying hands on people. Some people fell under the power of God, including all the worship singers. Sue, Katrina and I were now praying for others as well, as the local pastor directed us.

As the ministry time drew to a conclusion, the pastor asked if anyone had a testimony to share of what God had just done. Many shared, and the church was edified. An elder shared how God had shown him the church would expand and grow rapidly, and the church was encouraged.

After the testimonies, the pastor asked all the visitors to line up at the front, as the church wanted to "bless" us. Many people stepped forward to lay hands on us and pray. One of the young ladies from the worship team, along with an older lady, stood before me. In my spirit, it occurred to me that I was here in one of the richest places on earth because they loved and knew Jesus so passionately. This was the Body of Christ, standing before me, ministering to me. It was even more special than that: I recognized in their eyes the characteristics of Jesus, just as you can often see the likeness of a mother when looking at her daughter. Jesus Himself drew near to me—He was that recognizable in their faces!

The young lady beamed at me. They began to pray, and I closed my eyes. Soon I was laid out on the concrete with gentle hands being placed on my torso as they continued to pray. I couldn't understand their words in the natural, but in my spirit I was being blessed. I laughed and cried at the same time. It was all too beautiful, and I was grateful to God for allowing me to experience His presence and pleasure here in this humble setting. He is the Christ of the rubbish dump!

The service ended. We said our good-byes, yet spontaneous singing began as we filed out of the church into the smelly, cool night air. We climbed into the back of our truck, and then half the church crammed in also! We set off, and the singing resumed. It was joyful and passionate as we bumped our way up the hill. When we reached the main road, all the locals piled out and dispersed to their homes, and we continued on back to the Iris center at Zimpeto. Wow! What an experience!

August 2005 website visitors' blog postings

[Some more August postings]

Tim S: August 19, 2005 @ 6:07 A.M.

It would be easy to regret the wasted years of my own life (as I'm sure many could regret their own wasted years). But I now pray that I will be obedient to the Lord's voice so that the years ahead will be fruitful for His Kingdom.

The past month has been one of learning about a world I never knew before—one that I, like most in the affluent West, perhaps preferred to ignore. How easy it is to be seduced by the riches around us. How easy to let those thorns choke the word of the Gospel in our hearts. The most basic "necessities" in our lives would be beyond the dreams of the people you minister to.

How arrogant it would be to think I could pray for the believers in Mozambique with their bountiful riches in heaven. We need their prayers—to break our love of comfort and dependence on the riches of this world.

Brian C: August 20, 2005 @ 2:17 A.M.

I never thought I'd ever get a chance to see and experience anything like that which I've read about happening in Third World countries. But after hearing you speak this last February and March, I traveled with a team to Guyana, South America.

I am nobody special, a nobody from nowhere. But on the second night, I experienced an "open heaven" night, where everyone I touched got healed. I also learned that night, after seeing the look of amazement on an old Hindu woman's face when a tumor the size of a fist instantly disappeared, that all these miracles, signs and wonders are for the lost, the poor, the desperate, the people whose only hope is Jesus. I heard three months later from the pastor of that little island church that the little old lady's whole family got born again because of that one miracle.

The point is this: Yes, you can go and pray for the people of Africa, or anywhere else. All you need is the desire. If you go to where the poor and desperate are, with a ministry that believes in power evangelism, you will be used far beyond what you could ever hope for or imagine. It will not be because you are worthy, but because you went, and when you do, you will never be the same again.

Life principles: It's about love, not victory

There is a tendency for people to want to read only about the glory stories that come out of this revival that Jesus is leading, but there are gutsy stories, too. Unless you have the wider perspective of life here, then you will have a lopsided understanding of what God is doing. Often He teaches us through suffering about His glory-presence.

Once we had a meeting where we were praying for four of our kids who were really sick. They had measles and malaria, and in the end, two of them died. It happened just before we were due to go away for our annual staff retreat. That year we had a visiting speaker who had come to minister to our 160 staff. Bear in mind that the children who had died were *our* babies, *our* precious children. I was not at all impressed, then, when the speaker told us, "You all just need to laugh more!" I thought to myself, *I don't think the Lord is laughing at the moment.* In fact, I wanted to say, "I think your head is a little tilted, my friend!" But I had to make a choice. Was I going to get angry with this person and strangle them or was I going to bless them? I ended up blessing the person, of course, but it shook my world.

The very next Monday, I found myself lying facedown on a grass mat with the mother of one of the little girls who had died. I lay down with this woman and wept with her, holding her in my arms. It was then that God said to me, *Heidi, it's about love. It's not always about victory.* Our whole life cannot be about victory and glory—but it *must* be about love. Love is patient and kind and long-suffering. God's love is the kind of love that is extravagant, bottomless, ceaseless and endless. That's what you need when you are on the floor, holding a grieving mother.

We all need a download of holy love that so motivates us, it doesn't matter what people do to us—we just love them, regardless. If people offend you, like I was offended, you love them. If people spit in your face, you love them. If people falsely arrest you, you love them. When they put you in jail, you love them. When they beat you, you love them. We won over the garbage dump by love.

People hear our story and say, "Wow! What a powerful missionary story." Yes, we have thousands of churches; the blind see, the deaf hear, the dumb speak, the crippled walk, the dead get up. All these things happen over and again. But we also get beat up. Literally. Not with harsh words. We are literally beaten.

The first time I walked into the garbage dump, a guy named Vidal, who had a broken bottle in his hand, stuck it against my neck and said, "I'm going to slit your throat. What are you doing in my dump, you idiot white woman? I'm going to kill you now." I said to him, "Wait a minute. I'm so sorry. Just wait a second." And then I told him about Jesus dancing on the dump and putting clothes of beautiful gold and silver and blue and purple on the people in the dump. I told him I was walking with Jesus and said, "We put our hands upon your big bellies and they sink in. We put our hands upon your bullet wounds and they are healed. We put our hands upon your bleeding sores and they disappear and the lice die." I said to him, "I want to tell you about a feast that is ready and prepared, and God wants you to be there. Vidal, you are very beautiful, and you are invited to the head table."

After about half an hour of him grabbing me and threatening me, listening in between, he knelt in the garbage and began weeping. He said to me, "Could you please bring this man Jesus here because I want to meet Him." He had never heard His name before. Vidal was the first person to receive Christ on the rubbish dump, and now his entire village is saved. They were hungry, physically and spiritually, and we were offering them free food, physically and spiritually. They were very hungry. Are you? Jesus wants to give you more of Himself. He wants you to be immersed in His love so you can love others recklessly, completely, full of God's outrageous grace.

Chapter 5

Revival Fire for the Poor in Spirit

August–September 2005

Lilongwe, Malawi

News archive: posted September 8, 2005

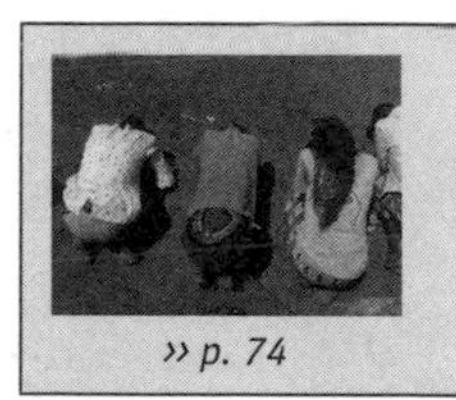

» p. 74

I'm back in Africa after weeks of conferences in the West, and I'm facing another kind of conference: a gathering of the poor, hungry, ragged, barefoot and sick from among our churches in the central region of Malawi. Carpets, air-conditioning and chandeliers have given way to dirt, blowing dust and the hot sun overhead. Hospitality rooms and coffee shops are replaced by iron pots of milled maize cooking over open wood fires. Hotel rooms with soft beds, clean sheets and warm showers have become grass mats under ripped and wind-blown black plastic coverings on a remote field with no electricity, water or relief from the night cold. Families huddle together in the dark to keep warm, without soap, toiletries or a change of clothes. Their threadbare shirts rip at a touch, and their teeth, hair and skin show the discolored ravages of malnutrition. They are weak. They hurt. And they long for ministry and love.

Malawi and northwest Mozambique are caught in yet more drought and famine. Four million people are in danger of starving.

The world hardly notices. Shipments from aid agencies don't make it to the remote villages where the need is greatest and where we have most of our churches. But we have called a "bush" conference to encourage our people, and Surpresa Sithole, one of our international directors, and I have come to preach the Gospel in this sea of need.

This has to be the poorest-looking conference the land has seen. Our property is off the main road outside the city of Lilongwe, a long journey on foot for many. We have a shaky platform of rough poles and boards, and we've strung some lights to use with a generator during meetings. There are no banners or signboards, no dignitaries in suits. As we set up and mix with the people, our clothes become covered with dirt. There is no parking lot full of vehicles and no handouts and no name tags. We are a band of human beings in the middle of nowhere, it seems, calling out to God for revival and the glory of His presence where all seems destitute and hopeless to the natural eye.

But this is what we live for, to preach the Good News to the poor and to bring life, love and joy to the saddest and heaviest of hearts. We present ourselves as instruments of righteousness to bring a foretaste of heaven into the least likely corners of the earth. We don't come with fame and fanfare but instead arrive in weakness, with nothing to preach but Jesus and Him crucified. Nothing less than the power of the cross will rescue and sustain these lives and hearts.

For three days we preach our hearts out, joined by David Morrison, our lead Iris missionary in Malawi. Hang on to Jesus! Never let Him go! Come to Him for everything. Don't throw away your faith. Bury yourself in His heart. Draw close to Him and He will draw close to you. And this unspeakably wonderful Savior of ours will freely give you the Kingdom. Don't be like unbelievers, who worry about everything, but pursue righteousness, peace and joy in the Holy Spirit, and you will have what you need. Nothing can separate us from the love of God—not famine, not poverty, not anything!

And so the people move forward in waves to kneel, worship and receive more of His grace. The Holy Spirit brings healing to bodies and hearts. Tears and laughter are released. Emotions are set free. Bowing and falling, rolling and shaking in the dirt, the hungry of all ages become filled to overflowing with God Himself. He knows how to love His beloved until they feel loved.

The people are encouraged and overjoyed. Their testimonies flow. I still feel utterly weak and inadequate, seeing their needs, but I grow in confidence that the Gospel will triumph in their lives. What will God do in response? Open the hearts of His people around the world and give them the opportunity to learn the heavenly art of love all the more. Our only job is to love—and if love is real at all, it is practical.

We have to go, but we promise more visits and conferences. We are cheered with enthusiasm and affection. I am praying that a supernaturally motivated and enabled wave of assistance from around the world will materialize out of the ever-increasing faith that we see before us—and that everything from weather patterns to politics will be transformed by an unstoppable spread of revival fire.

Malawi is hungry

David Morrison: posted September 1, 2005 @ 2:12 P.M.

Iris conference in Lilongwe

We recently hosted the first central region conference in two years. Our ministry team from Bangula, including our commissioners, Bible school teachers, choir and southern region overseers, set off from Bangula at 5:00 A.M. to begin the eight-hour journey to Lilongwe. We were joined by Surpresa Sithole and Rolland Baker, who flew in for the conference. We were also encouraged by a team of missionaries and nationals from Dondo, Mozambique, who drove for sixteen hours in order to come and assist us.

On our arrival we encountered excited men, women and children who were so happy to be sought after and given attention. They came to Lilongwe on trucks from the surrounding villages in the bush where they live very humbly and, right now, without much food. They didn't bring much with them, for they have very little. They were just content to be in a place where they could learn more about Jesus. They didn't care that they had to sleep together in families outside on mats on the dirt. All they wanted was to see Jesus. They were hungry for the One who gave up His life so that they might live. Nothing else seemed to matter. This was their special time, and special they knew they were.

Our churches in this region have really struggled in the past with poor leadership. But now, with new leaders in place, our churches are experiencing growth. Our newly appointed committee of pastors here have proven themselves to be faithful workers. They demonstrate love and unity toward one another, and their first concern is clearly their people. At the conference the people danced, worshiped and listened to teaching under the intense sunshine as blasts of dust and sand carried by the wind beat at them on the ground. When given opportunity for prayer ministry, they unreservedly came forward, humbling themselves before their Lord. The Lord loved on them by the power of the Holy Spirit. All they wanted was a touch from Him, and they got it. Some were moved to tears, others joy. Young and old, they knelt before the Lord, crying out with tears pouring down their cheeks and faces either turned toward heaven or planted down in the dirt.

One day during the ministry time, I kept close to a ten-year-old boy who was clearly being ministered to by the Holy Spirit. He was on bended knees with his face to the ground, shaking and sometimes crying. I kept on praying for him. Afterward, with an interpreter, I asked him to explain what was happening as he knelt on the ground. He said that he wasn't sure, but he was thankful to God because now he felt much freer and lighter. In Matthew 11:28, Jesus invites all who are weary and burdened to come to Him. Life is very difficult here in this land, even for ten-year-old boys. So they rejoice in Jesus whose yoke leads to living freely and lighter.

Children are filling our homes! Timothy was hungry for a home and a family to love him. We arrived at Timothy's broken-down home in a Bangula village to pick him up. He had already been briefed by his oldest brother that he was going to have a new family. I thought that a small boy would be a little apprehensive of such a change. My prediction proved false. Instead, upon our arrival, seven-year-old Timothy quickly embraced us with hugs and a huge smile. He was so willing and ready to come and begin a new life in one of our recently completed children's homes at the Iris missions base.

Timothy's parents died of sickness on the same day earlier this year. For months now, Timothy has been living alone with his two older brothers. There are no relatives here to take them in and no neighbors able to help. Timothy's oldest brother (aged nineteen years) has tried very hard with little bits of part-time work to earn money for food. They have also been selling off items from their home, little by little, in desperation for food. The second born, aged seventeen, has a place at secondary school but had to drop out when no money was available to pay for school fees. The older boys are too old to come to us, but we will not leave them alone. We have already provided them food and will be sponsoring the younger one through school.

It was a joyous occasion bringing Timothy home. He slept on a new mattress with sheets on a bed covered with a mosquito net. He ate well and was loved by his new house parents, Nsitu and Fanny. Everything was new for him—even the instructions on how to use the toilet and shower. The first night was so exciting for him that he woke up at midnight ready to begin his day. So, he got showered (again) and put on his school uniform. It took some convincing by house dad, Nsitu, to get Timothy back into bed for several more hours. He eventually fell back asleep, very clean and safe in his new home.

This is a time of great excitement for our pastors. Some have returned for their third year of training. They love coming back to school. I'm sure partly it is because we provide them with three meals a day as well as soap, toothpaste and a blanket. But I know that more than that, they arrive looking forward to meeting their Lord and Savior once again in a new way as they grow deeper in faith and understanding of the Scriptures. They really are hungry to be more like Jesus. We've invited our senior leaders from throughout the country to receive the first of the third-year courses. We want to pour into them and let God love more life into them so they can help us train the others. Since Joanna [David's wife] and I are the only educators here, it makes for a heavy term of teaching. But we, too, are hungry for God to continue His work, changing these men from the inside out.

Hungry for food

Today, millions of people in Malawi do not have enough food to eat, and the situation is only going to get worse. There is simply not enough food to go around. We are now feeding three thousand of the most desperate—the widows, elderly, crippled and blind. They come to us on the fifteenth of each month for food distribution. Hundreds repeatedly come between distribution dates, hungry, with nowhere else to go.

We give them what we have, and they are satisfied for the time being. Yesterday we gave away twenty tons of maize. These days we are currently buying up as much maize as we can get our hands on. That's not always an easy task—our suppliers are traveling great distances to farmers deep into Mozambique. Then, one fifty-kilogram bag of maize at a time, they carry them back to Malawi. It's a long and strenuous process that contributes in part to the high cost of maize. The market price is now three times more than it usually is at harvest time. Many simply don't have money and cannot buy. Therefore, they harvest lily bulbs that grow in the river—the crocodile-infested river. The bulbs are then dried, milled and cooked like porridge. It doesn't taste very good, but it fills their stomachs.

Malawi has experienced the worst harvest in ten years, and there are reports suggesting that 4.2 million Malawians need assistance now. We believe it! We see the signs of disaster all around us. The next harvest is still eight months away. We are seeing more and more children with swollen stomachs. People are getting thinner. Every day people who don't know where else to turn come to us. We are frequently hearing from pastors who are walking great distances from their bush villages to describe the desperation of people back home. It is very difficult being surrounded by such great suffering. Even so, we keep moving forward with our faith in Jesus, who can multiply food and can fill and satisfy every life. In the midst of suffering we continue to declare Jesus' words when He said, "I am the bread of life. He who comes to me will never go hungry, and he who believes in me will never be thirsty" [John 6:35]. So please join us in prayer for the hungry in Malawi: "O Lord, give us today our daily bread."

Heidi's blog entry
September 2005

Thank you for praying for me and keeping in touch. It is a joy to know that you care about us. We had a tremendous life-changing time with our Bible college and missions school in Cabo Delgado, Mozambique, this year.

» p. 74 » p. 75 » p. 75 » p. 76

We just had a graduation with over four hundred students. The international students studied with the Mozambican students.

They cheerfully lived without running water or electricity. They were truly the fragrance of Christ Jesus in Pemba. So many of these awesome students are my heroes. They are wholly given, laid-down lovers of Jesus.

The Lord has opened the hearts of the Makua and the Makondi tribes in Pemba. Tens of thousands have come to know beautiful Jesus. On a recent Sunday morning as we all danced and sang in our sandy green tent, an older Makondi woman with a beautifully tattooed face gave her life to Jesus. She ran up in the dust and told me how her daughter who was completely out of her mind was healed in church the Sunday before. Another lady jumped and screamed, "I can see, I can see!" as Jesus opened her eyes. She, too, wanted to follow the Lord!

We are so thankful to be taking in new children almost daily. They are full orphans from the villages in the bush. Jesus said, *Take them all*, so this month we have taken over a hundred new children in Mozambique and Indonesia. I want to thank you for your love, prayers and support for these amazing children. Words will never be enough to thank you for remembering all of us.

Much love in Jesus,
Heidi

Life principles: The face of revival

God is not about using the mighty, but the willing. He is not into using amazing people, just ones who are prepared to lay their lives down to Him. God is not looking for extraordinary, exceptionally gifted people, just laid-down lovers of Jesus who will carry His glory with transparency and not take it for themselves.

In Luke 10:25 we read about a wise man, a well-educated expert on the Law, who stood up and challenged Jesus. He wanted to test Jesus, so he asked Him, "What must I do to inherit eternal life?" The question, in and of itself, was a good one. But Jesus, being predisposed to answer a question with another question, shot straight back at him with: "What is written in the Law? . . . How do you read it?" (verse 26).

The Law expert already knew the answer. He replied, " 'Love the Lord your God with all your heart and with all your soul and with all your strength and with all your mind'; and, 'Love your neighbor as yourself' " (verse 27). This man knew how to answer Jesus' question, but he did not know what he ought to do about it. He was unable to comprehend what it meant in practical terms.

This man who spoke to Jesus did not get it. He spoke out the words, but he missed the point. Jesus responded to him, saying, "Yes, you've answered correctly," but then He added one more little statement: "Do this and you will live" (verse 28). This is the thing that the Law expert really needed to understand. And this is the part we need to get if we want to see revival. If we love God with all our beings, we will live! If we do this, we will see revival. If we do this, the Gospel will go forth. This is the simplicity of Jesus' message.

The power of God, the presence of God, the multiplication of the Gospel, is as simple as this: a physical demonstration of the love of God. We have overcomplicated our message, thinking we were being wise. We have analyzed the Gospel to death until it doesn't work anymore! We have made it so intensely difficult to understand that we have theologized, theorized and strategized ourselves into a corner. We have not understood that the Gospel is as simple as this: love, love, love, love, love!

The Gospel is about passion. Do you understand that when you are a passionate lover of God, He will do anything for you? When you are madly in love with someone, you will do anything for them, won't you? For example, Rolland hates herbal tea. He thinks it's disgusting. But, when he came to see me when we were dating, I would often say to him, "Would you like some herbal tea?" And he would say, "Oh yes, thank you!" The day after we got married, he told me, "I hate herbal tea. It's horrible! I can't believe you would ever drink that!" Amazed, I said to him, "But you drank it for months when you came over to visit me!" Rolland replied, "Yes, but I was just so in love!"

People who are in love do things like that. They don't care. They don't care when they get shot at or when their heads get banged against a wall. They don't care when people put knives to their throats. They don't care when the Marxists are firing their machine guns in the air. They don't care because they are in love! Love is what is drives us forward. We are not driven through slavery or a desire to be somebody, because we already know we are children of the Most High God. It doesn't matter what anyone thinks of us. It doesn't matter what we look like or what the world says. We are adopted sons and daughters of God, so in love that we will do anything for Him!

Passion leads to compassion

I get into some wild spots at times, but nothing I do is difficult. It's not difficult because I am driven by love. I am compelled and motivated by love. It is my passion for Jesus that causes me to pour compassion into others. That's the Gospel—a passion that births compassion.

All fruitfulness flows from intimacy—and it is intimacy unto a harvest. Intimacy has to be for a purpose. If we want to embrace our Father's heart, then we must know that our Father's heart's desire is for His house to be full. The Father looks out at all the orphans of the world and wants them to be loved, accepted, welcomed home. When I stop to pick up an orphan off the street, it is a prophetic act that reflects the Father's heart.

The King of Glory is looking for servant-lovers who will bring in the poor, the crippled, the blind and the lame and fill up His house. He is looking for servant-lovers who know who they are and are not afraid—so full of love that *fear* is not a word in their vocabulary. Radical lovers of God move in radical compassion!

The expert of the Law who questioned Jesus couldn't accept the simplicity and directness of His words. "No, no," he said, "surely you don't mean that. There must be something else? It can't possibly be that simple." He was unable to comprehend the simplicity of the truth that the whole of life flows out of a reckless love for the Father—that such a love spills out of us and touches everyone we meet.

The man tried another line of questioning: "Wait a minute, Jesus, who is my neighbor?" (see Luke 10:29). Another good question. Who is our neighbor? Is it the famine victim in Malawi? The person in prison in Afghanistan? The person who lives under a bridge in Mozambique? The person who lives down the street from you and works in Kmart? The answer is, all of these people. But because Jesus knew that the man would not understand the depth and reach of a simple statement like "Everyone!" He began to tell a story.

The story of the Good Samaritan is one that has so impacted my life, because I am challenged to live it every day. I'm not saying that to make any grand claim, but, for me, this story illustrates the simplicity of the Gospel, and it has come alive inside me. I believe it is as simple as Jesus says it is.

A guy is walking on the road that runs from Jerusalem to Jericho when he falls into the hands of robbers. They strip him of all his clothes and beat him, leaving him half dead on the roadside. Here is a man who is suffering, who has been beaten and abused and who is slowly dying with no one to help him. He is not lovely or attractive; he is bloody and naked. How will people respond to him?

I've walked that road from Jerusalem to Jericho. It is a descending road that is dusty and not very wide. It is impossible, naturally speaking, to miss someone lying at the side of the road. You would almost have to step over them. You could not kid yourself that you didn't see a dying man there.

This man was out on the dusty road in the heat when along came a priest. The priest, a man of God, couldn't stop because he was on his way to a church-growth conference and he was running late. He was on his way to learn how to grow his congregation and to look at different strategies to make it happen. He had a lot to do, and so he hurried past the dying, bleeding man. He was a blind priest. His eyes were open, but he could not see the face of revival. He could not see what was before him because he was too busy deciding how to grow his church.

Sometimes we cannot see and don't want to see because we are blinded. We need eye salve to put on our eyes. We cry out for revival, and yet God says, "I want to open your eyes so that you can see what is before you. Revival has a face and a name. It lies bleeding on the roadside."

The next guy who walks down the road is busy praying in the Spirit and is on his way to rehearse with his worship band. They are going to cut a great CD of worship songs. He is gifted to lead others in worship to God, but he is a blind Levite. Boy, can he sing, but he can't see! All he is thinking about is his worship band and recording his CD. He refuses to see the guy lying beaten and naked on the road because he does not want to deal with it. It's too simple, too direct. Surely you don't have to stop for *everyone*? Anyway, it's not his "calling." He is too busy doing other things.

When God let this message burn in my heart, He told me, *Heidi, I want you to stop for them all.* It was a prophetic statement. When I first arrived in Mozambique, I was on my own. Rolland was finishing writing his doctoral thesis. I went out with a one-way ticket and no possessions. After two days I ran out of money. I was sitting alone on the curbside, wondering what to do, and God met with me there and told me, *This is where I have sent you. You are going to see revival here, and all I want you to do is stop for the one.*

So that is all I did. I didn't have some strategic plan of how to reach the city by 20XX. I didn't have it all figured out in my mind. All I knew was that God had told me to stop for the one. He told me, *Heidi, I want you to* see. *I want the passion I put inside you to be so full that compassion flows out of you.* So I began to sit with the poor and pick up little children and love them.

One day I picked up Gito [sounds like "Geetoo"]. Gito had been beaten and raped and was dying there on the street. He was a skinny little kid who had been violated, abused and left for dead. He was dying on the road under an overpass, and I sat with him and held him in my arms and loved him. He had been raped so many times that he had AIDS. I held him in my arms and said, "Come home with me, Gito." His was the face of revival. There was no snazzy plan, no slick brochures. Later, God totally healed Gito of AIDS. We received the negative tests back from the doctor. There are thousands more orphans like Gito. They are the face of revival. Jesus said, "Whatever you do to the least of these you do to Me." I have seen the face of Jesus in the faces of the street children. I have seen His eyes looking at me through their eyes.

When you stop for one person and pour the compassion of God into them and tell them they are adopted, it has a dramatic effect on them. We don't call our center an orphanage, because all those kids are adopted by the Father. They are the happiest children I know and they are full of joy. Do you want to see revival? Do you want to see the love of God poured out in your city? Well, God is saying, "See!" He wants to impart His heart to you in such a way that you become full of His passion. He wants you to be so full of His love that nobody can stop you from being compassionate to every person who crosses your path every day of your life.

But do not be fooled by their disguises. Many on the road who are bleeding, desperate and dying are well dressed. They work in banks and offices and attend universities. They do not look poor; they look affluent, but they are wretched, naked and dying. Can you see them?

Lilongwe, Malawi, photo

Bowing before Jesus in the Malawi dirt

Heidi's blog entry for September 2005 photos

1. We serve beans and rice for lunch every day for pastors, students, children and visitors at the missions school

2. Pastors and missions students praying for new believers in our Pemba tent

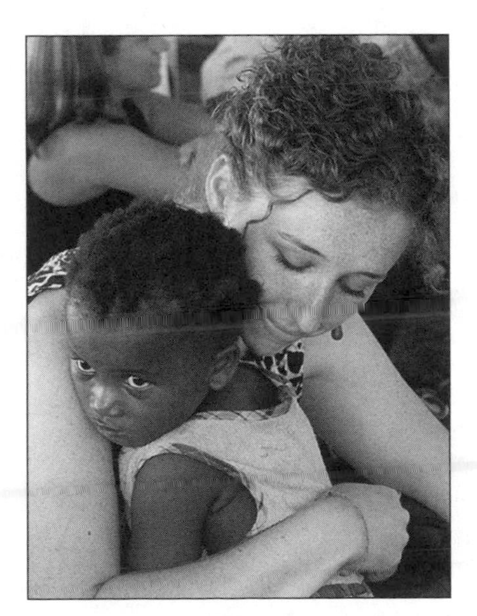

3. The missions school offers lots of chances to hug kids

4. Our missions-school graduation class in Pemba

Chapter 6

The Miracle of Suffering

September–October 2005

Update from Rolland

Open heaven over Cabo Delgado

News archive: posted September 8, 2005

Moslem leaders are admitting that this northernmost province on the coast of Mozambique, once considered "unreachable" by missiologists, is being lost to Christians. The development of our base and missions school on the largest available piece of property in the port city of Pemba has caused a major stir. The Gospel is advancing whole villages at a time as the Holy Spirit's power is poured out.

How does this happen? Here is one example. Felito Utuie, a 22-year-old evangelist we have nurtured in the Lord, was trying to get the Moslem chief of a village to grant permission for an outreach. The chief repeatedly refused. Felito told him that Jesus would heal the sick. Finally, the chief asked, "If you come, will I see that happen?" "Yes!" Felito answered simply. So the chief agreed to a meeting in his village.

On the night of the outreach, the meeting began with a very quiet, open atmosphere, unlike some gatherings we have where at first we face loud demonic disruptions. Felito preached the pure, simple Gospel and asked, "Who recognizes their need of a Savior?" Voices cried out in the dark, "I want forgiveness! I want forgiveness!" A great noise arose as the people pleaded for salvation and streamed forward to pray. Then Felito announced that he and his team would pray for the sick. Healings occurred one after another. A mother brought her eight-year-old boy who was deaf, and he was instantly healed. Felito asked the chief, "Do you see?" Immediately, the chief asked for the microphone and told his own people, "This is real! No man can do this! Only God can do this! Bring more of the sick! Bring all the sick!"

One man brought his little seven-year-old daughter who was totally blind. She received prayer, and her father urgently asked her, "Do you see?" And then tears began streaming down his face as his daughter looked up and saw his face for the first time in her life! And the healings continued that night.

All this last year our outreaches have been frequently bearing this kind of fruit. We don't preach long or get complicated. The people respond in simple faith, and as soon as they see Jesus is real and will touch them miraculously, they want Him! They want salvation, they want a church, they want a pastor, now! Their chiefs beg us, "Don't leave us! You can't leave us like this! We've never seen miracles like this! You have to come back and teach us!"

Heidi especially has received a special anointing for the deaf, blind and lame, and sees them healed at nearly every outreach. Once she prayed late at night for a crippled and blind man who was not healed right away. But she told the village to send a runner to tell her as soon as he was healed. The following day she was with a good Moslem friend and leading businessman in town when a runner ran breathlessly up to the window of the car they were in. "He is healed! He can walk and see!" The runner had just run for seven hours to tell her. In tears and awe, our Moslem friend cried, "Pray for me! Pray for me now!"

A missions school on the mission field

In August we completed the first session of our Holy Given: Iris International School of Missions in Pemba. An intense challenge and adventure in faith, it tested us to the extreme in every way. Initially through the vision of Heidi and our close friend in ministry over many years, Lesley-Anne Leighton, the school produced rich fruit against all odds. Other Holy Given sessions are being offered at locations around the world under Lesley's direction. Here the idea is to offer teaching not only in an atmosphere soaked and dripping with the Holy Spirit, but one situated in an extremely needy, difficult and spiritually desperate Third World environment where missions can be practiced daily!

Around two hundred students arrived in June from all over the world to face real mission-field hardships: no electricity, running water, Western toilets or enough accommodation. Our PDF flyer for the school was downloaded ten thousand times from our website. We initially planned on admitting one hundred students, but kept adding more as people applied right up to the first week of school. For months we were constructing housing in preparation for the school, but the typical delays and frustrations of such projects in Africa left us far behind schedule. Students ended up in tents and crowded together in our few completed dorm rooms. We met in a large tent often blowing in the wind near the ocean, sat on plastic chairs and spent much time daily at the altar in the dirt on grass mats. A stream of well-known, revival-oriented visiting speakers fed us richly, more than we could contain and absorb. Every day the Holy Spirit would fall on us, reaching deep into our hearts and transforming us from glory to glory into the likeness of Jesus.

Several times a week the students would divide into teams and head to the villages to preach the Gospel and heal the sick. Many who had never before been far from home or experienced anything like this were stunned and thrilled to see miracles before their eyes throughout their stay. Most were grateful for the opportunity to endure some of the hardships that are common to the poor in most of the world. Our students grew close to us and each other, many wishing they could stay and crying at the thought of having to leave. More than half the students want to continue in missions in some capacity with Iris Ministries somewhere in the world. We are overjoyed at the stream of testimonies we have received of lives being changed forever by exposure to the Kingdom here in Mozambique.

One month later: Urgent prayer request for Heidi

Posted October 2, 2005

I (Rolland) finally got home to Pemba after five flights, but on arrival had to turn around immediately and take Heidi to an emergency clinic in Maputo, and now we are on our way to a hospital in South Africa. She has an extremely dangerous, life-threatening staph infection that has resurfaced after she was hospitalized with the same thing three weeks ago in Malaysia. This type of staph is highly drug-resistant and in Malaysia was affected by only one kind of antibiotic in the world. Heidi has been taking that antibiotic for these three weeks, but now the infection has flared up severely and is out of control. She has had this infection a number of times over the years, passing it on to me once. Each time it gets worse and harder to treat. Now it is spreading quickly and she is in great pain. We and all at our base in Pemba are praying, and now we are asking for our friends around the world to pray and join with us in trusting Jesus with all our hearts.

Much love in Him,
Rolland

Note from Heidi
Posted October 5, 2005 @ 5:19 A.M.

Dear friends,
I never felt so loved by the Body of Christ. I'm overwhelmed by your kindness. Thank you so much for praying for me. This is the second time I've been hospitalized in less than a month. I have been diagnosed with Methicillin-resistant Staphylococcus infection. I'm now on the last super-antibiotic. The doctor told me I'll be in the hospital here for fourteen days. However, I am positive Jesus is healing me and I'll be out of here in no time. I feel His love and presence in my room. I'm going to make some changes in my lifestyle and take more time to rest. Here are some Scriptures I have been encouraged by lately:

> And He said, "My Presence will go with you, and I will give you rest."
>
> Exodus 33:14, NKJV

> On God my salvation and my glory rest;
> The rock of my strength, my refuge is in God.
>
> Psalm 62:7, NASB

> He who dwells in the shelter of the Most High
> will rest in the shadow of the Almighty.
>
> Psalm 91:1

Much love in Jesus,
Heidi

Rolland's blog entry
Posted October 7, 2005 @ 10:15 P.M.

Please continue to pray.

Heidi's lab tests show that she has the most resistant form of staph. She is receiving the most powerful antibiotic available by IV drip and will be on that for some time. In some ways, her health has started to show improvement, but she is taking action to build up her immune system with probiotic health supplements. Her body is in quite a weakened state after being on strong antibiotics for so long, but Jesus has given her a fighting spirit and she is asking for continued prayer.

Much, much love and huge appreciation to all!
Rolland

Response to blog entry
Pastors Gary and Laura K: October 2, 2005 @ 3:18 A.M.

Jesus has heard your prayers and the cries of the harvesters from around the world, crying out on your behalf for healing. . . . He is renewing your strength. He's mounting you up to prepare you for the next level Jesus is taking you to. It will be glorious!

Blessings on you, your family and ministry.

Note from Heidi
Posted October 8, 2005 @ 9:05 A.M.

Thank you again for your amazing love and prayers. Thank you for standing with me and believing with me. I feel so much of the love of God through you. I am still in the hospital on Zyvoxid and Vancomycin IV drips. The Lord has spoken to me and I'm going to the "Soaking in God's Glory" conference. As I'm resting in God's presence, He is downloading revelation on carrying His glory. . . . The nurses are coming to me, asking for prayer because the presence of God is so strong in my room.

Much, much love in Jesus,
Heidi

Response to blog posting
Joette C: October 10, 2005 @ 3:00 P.M.

We rejoice at the Lord's faithfulness and merciful healing touch. We are asking and believing for the staph infection to be eradicated, never to return! We also have been believing that all around you would see and know the huge love of our Father and be drawn to Him. Praise Him for His faithfulness. . . . We believe that the Lord's plans for your life are not yet accomplished, and we are standing in faith that you will live to see them fulfilled.

Update from Heidi
Posted October 14, 2005

Again I want to thank you for your amazing response in prayer. I have never felt so lifted up and loved by the Body of Christ. God turned the enemy's plan around for His good. A dear friend sent me a Scripture: "Nevertheless to remain in the flesh is more needful for you" (Philippians 1:24, NKJV). Those who know me well, know I often long to depart and be with the Lord. I am so in love with Him. Several very powerful, life-changing trips to heaven in the Spirit have caused my heart to desire to stay there. However, I see the lost Bride and know that I shall remain and continue with you all, the beautiful Body of Christ, for your progress and joy in the faith (see Philippians 1:25). I want to live and see multitudes of radical, laid-down, wholly given lovers released on the earth to find and bring to Jesus His lost Bride. I will live to see the Makua tribe in great numbers worshiping the Lamb upon the throne, who is so worthy of adoration. I will live to see radical, supernatural healing on the earth. I will live to demonstrate my faith in my beloved Jesus. I will live to bring millions to my King Jesus!

I'm still in the hospital. I am full of faith. Many of my children called yesterday and cried on the phone. They said, "Mom, we love you! You have to come home now!" When the doctor told me he believed I should not return to Mozambique because it was too dangerous for my health, I laughed and felt a very powerful, holy fight come upon me! I will go home to Pemba, Cabo Delgado, soon, and hold all my beautiful children! I will return to this fabulous harvest!

You are precious to me, and you are loved.

Resting in the arms of my Father,
Heidi

Report from Heidi
Posted October 26, 2005

Thank you for praying for me and believing God with me. The Lord has done marvelous things for me. I felt Jesus told me to go and preach in Toronto and that He would heal me.

I saw a specialist in South Africa last Wednesday. He said the antibiotics were able to keep the infection from spreading as long as I was on the IV drip, but they were not able to kill the MRSA bacteria. My only hope, according to the doctor, was to go to the States and check into a university medical center where they would operate to cut out and drain the infection. He told me that after a month in the hospital they might be able to make progress.

I believed Jesus had another plan. I booked a flight with Rolland and told the doctors that I was checking out to see a top specialist in Toronto, Canada. I think you all know Him! When I arrived late on Thursday afternoon, I was very weak and in a lot of pain. I had to go almost immediately to the conference to speak. I worshiped in my weakness and believed Jesus for a miracle. When I got up to preach from the book of Zechariah, I felt the supernatural power of God flowing through me. The infection was literally being healed as I was speaking. At the end I felt Jesus call me to dance with Him. He poured His love and power through me!

The next morning I got up early and went for a jog! On Saturday I went to a famous hospital in California and showed the emergency doctors all my lab reports and the specialist's letter from South Africa. They got ready to admit me, but I asked them to please look at the "infection" first. The doctor said, "This is healing up well. You won't need an operation." Then I told him what Jesus did for me. He said, "Praise the Lord! This is amazing!"

I am still committed to changing my lifestyle and spending even more time to rest in His glory-presence. I am forever grateful for all your love and prayers. Jesus did a mighty miracle!

Love,
Heidi

Life principles: The miracle of suffering

Early on in our ministry we lost all our buildings (all 55 of them) and were left homeless. We were at the most desperate place we've ever been. We had nothing at all. Yet it was at that moment I suddenly thought, *Who cares! In fact, who cares if we literally starve to death—us and all our children?* I had come to a place where I realized that God's presence was worth more to me than life itself. This is not a joke or an exaggeration. I am seriously saying that Jesus' presence is worth more to me than anything—that His love and His precious blood are worth more to me than life itself. I don't see the point of prosperity and well-being in life if all it does is distract you from Jesus!

What was surprising to me was that it was when we reached this lowest place ever that all heaven started to break open for us. When we were suffering, God manifested Himself in a very real way. In the West we don't like the idea of "suffering" very much. We would prefer that no one had to suffer—especially those who are in Christ. But the fact is, when we began suffering, and when hundreds of children fell on their faces worshiping God and crying out to Him, it was then the miracles began to flow. What food we had was miraculously multiplied, power came from heaven that supernaturally sustained us and many other miracles occurred. The stuff that happened when we lost everything and had no backup plan and nothing to eat or drink was amazing. When we literally had no ability to live, no way to function in the natural, God came like a cloud and took care of us.

Sometimes suffering can be a wonderful thing! Maybe you need to hear that. Suffering can bring you closer to God. Of course, it's never our first choice, but when it happens it can birth either bitterness in us or compassion. I was sick for a number of years. Not just a little sick, but super sick. I was in a lot of pain all the time. I couldn't walk for long periods and often couldn't even lie still and read. At other times, when I managed to get up and walk about, I would have to hold on to the pulpit in order to preach because I was so weak. Guess what happened to me during that time? The type A, driven personality that I had was ripped out of me because I was physically unable to "push through" like I always used to. Through that suffering, a great compassion was birthed in me—a compassion for anyone who is hurting.

Don't be afraid of suffering. The immense love of Jesus is far bigger than anything you will face in life. Surrender yourself to Him completely, and none of the challenges that life throws at you will ever look the same again.

Chapter 7

Worldwide Hunger for God

October–November 2005

Update from Rolland

We are hearing a cry for revival and the work of the Holy Spirit coming from all over the world, and especially where there is great suffering, hardship and persecution. Email comes to us in a stream from across Africa and Asia, desperately requesting visits, ministry, conferences, teaching, guidance, impartation and material help. Heidi and I, and our existing ministry staff, are responding with all the strength God gives us, but we issue to you an invitation to join hands with us. The Lord of the harvest could bring the harvest in alone by His own might, but He chooses to share His divine nature and glory with us. Enter with us into a world of love, rest and companionship even while buffeted fiercely on all sides by evil storms. In Him we are more than conquerors, shielded through faith by God's power until Jesus is fully revealed. We are ready to carry His glory into the darkness wherever the love of God is wanted!

In addition to the various nations of southeast Africa where we have been working since 1995, we are in various stages of being established as a government-registered, recognized ministry in Congo, Indonesia, Sudan, Sierra Leone and others. Angola,

Liberia and various countries of North Africa are next on our list. Our ministry contacts and lead pastors in all these nations are urgently inviting visiting teams, speakers and those with badly needed practical gifts of all kinds.

Our orphanage on the island of Nias in Indonesia is thriving, and we are adding involvement with another orphanage in Bali, where Heidi and I first began our ministry together in 1980. Both these works need much attention, and we especially invite the participation of nearby Aussies and Kiwis. We are prophetically focused on another "tsunami of the Holy Spirit" in Indonesia to follow up the wonderful revival there of the '60s and '70s.

In most places where we have begun ministry, the devil has caused huge damage, and the existing Christians are heroically maintaining and advancing in spite of hardships that I cannot adequately express. As one example among many, I quote an email from our Pastor Joseph in Bukavu, DR Congo:

> We wanted also to report to you one tragedy of genocide that occurred to one village called Fendula and Ninja where we have a church, and our Pastor Badesire Munjombola just lost his wife as the Nterahamwe Rwandese combatants who have been in that area now attacked the population and set ablaze houses, and 47 people have been reported killed, and hundreds who ran for safety now are without shelter, food, medicine, and we still have others in hospital. We went there with Sifa and prayed with them. Please continue to pray for families that lost their own and for our pastor and church members among others.

This is just one small event in a war-torn country where bombs and mortar fire have demolished one out of three homes. There are no factories at all. Jobs are scarce, and every day the Congolese people struggle to survive until the next meal.

Many of our missions-school students are strongly called to these countries where we are already involved, and we urge you and others to stay in close contact and keep looking to Jesus with us for further direction and provision. We will establish special mailing lists for each field and group of interested missionaries.

Opposition aroused

Some who hear us in conferences may come away with the impression that we lead a charmed, tribulation-free life of endless miracles! We do prefer to give Jesus and His glorious power most of the attention in our ministry, but it may encourage you to know that, like Paul, we are jars of clay who glory also in our weakness. When we are weak, then we are strong (see 2 Corinthians 12:10). We do encounter fierce, demonic opposition, and its intensity is almost incomprehensible. This Mozambican province where we live has been a pagan, occultic stronghold for centuries, and the evil we encounter shocks us over and over. Our time, energy, funds and resources are viciously attacked and drained as the devil aims to turn our hearts away from this great revival in which God has graciously placed us.

Together with Paul, we understand that these things happen "that we might not rely on ourselves but on God, who raises the dead" (2 Corinthians 1:9). We resist the devil by overcoming evil with good and by resting in Jesus with all the more faith and childlike joy. We cannot lose while secure in His heart. We have no need to shield ourselves, but we entrust our souls to a faithful Creator in doing what is right (see 1 Peter 4:19). The God who has raised at least 53 people from the dead among our churches in Africa will also renew and refresh us with His incomparable power. He will not fail us; we are His workmanship!

Feeding the hungry

David Morrison: posted October 30, 2005 @ 7:47 P.M.

It's sunrise and people begin their journey from all over the Bangula region to the Iris Ministries food-distribution center. Some walk for hours with empty stomachs and bare feet. They are hopeful that at the end of their journey under the intense sun, they will receive food. Those who come are desperate. Hundreds and hundreds of widows and elderly come. Many of these older people are left with orphaned grandchildren and find it impossible to find enough food for themselves, let alone the children. One by one, people come—some in wheelchairs, others at a snail's pace with canes. The blind walk with guidance from a young child, usually in tattered clothes and hungry. These are the ones we call "vulnerable," and they need our help. Approximately 2,500 people gather, and still hundreds more in days to follow.

It was a scramble, but thanks to assistance from people around the world, money was sent quickly from Iris Ministries Canada to purchase maize that arrived just in time. Praise be to God! The first of three trucks arrived at 8:00 A.M., giving the pastors from the Bible school time to off-load in preparation for distribution. Meanwhile, those gathering had begun to worship the Lord with singing and dancing. They had seen the truck and were filled with joy.

Soon Paulendo, one of our pastors at the Bible school, preached to the crowd about Jesus, the Bread of Life. The Holy Spirit was at work, drawing people to our Savior. The response was amazing, as many came forward to receive Jesus as their Lord and Savior. They came to receive food to relieve the hunger pains, but, as well, they met Jesus, who removes their sins and fills them with new life. Others came forward repenting, handing in their witchcraft paraphernalia. Our team of pastors from the Bible school prayed for everyone, not leaving anyone out.

After the time of worship, teaching and ministry, people were called from the list to receive food. There were no fights, nor even pushing, just patient people waiting under the hot sun for their names to be called. Everyone received twelve kilograms of enriched maize flour and they were so happy. Twelve kilograms translates into approximately sixty servings of *nsima*, which means two people can eat once a day for a month.

Many thanks to everyone who helped us feed the hungry here in Malawi. Our pastors at the Bible school commented on how wonderful it was that people from around the world heard the cry of the hungry in Malawi and have contributed funds to make this possible. They kept saying, "God bless them! We must pray for those who have sent all this food." I wish that all of you were able to experience what I saw this day. Unfortunately, that isn't possible, but at least you can appreciate a little taste from this report.

We praise God for providing enough food to allow us to feed all the people who came to us, and there was even enough food left over to sustain those who have larger families.

Malawi conference

[Reflections from Nikki Wheeler, Iris missionary]

Our center in Malawi, in the tiny town of Bangula, was having its regional conference. I was at this same conference last year, before I had even started working for Iris. I still have the same journal, and I flipped back to where I had written of my experiences. Things have changed so much. Actually, the style of the conference has stayed the same—it's my attitude toward it that has changed! I will let you read some excerpts of what I wrote then and my thoughts now.

Rolland, Heidi and I were flying down to Bangula in Rolland's Cessna 206. It's a fairly short flight, about four hours, with a quick stopover in Blantyre to pass through immigration—and stock up on cookies and ice cream! Malawi law does not permit anyone to fly [take off] after official sunset. Everyone has to be in the air by 5:45 P.M. We arrived at 5:30 P.M., which meant we had only fifteen minutes to get our passports stamped, refuel the plane and take off before airport officials would ground us for the night. Then Heidi went into the only shop at the airport! About twenty minutes later we finally got into the plane, and the tower gave Rolland special permission to leave. The flight from Blantyre to Bangula is only about thirty minutes, so they allowed us to leave on the condition that Rolland called the tower and let them know that we had landed safely.

The scenery is beautiful, so rugged and mountainous. From the air you can see small farms on the hillsides, and they look lush and green. It is hard to imagine that this area is the most impoverished part of Malawi. There are more people dying of starvation here than anywhere else in Africa—droughts and rains at the wrong time have completely wrecked this part of the country.

The sun was gone, and it was getting dark. Rolland had called Mo [David Morrison] from the airport and asked him to start clearing the runway: "Activating goat-on-runway detector!" In the distance we could see the two "pin-scourers'" [Pinzgauer—a Swiss Army off-road vehicle] headlights flashing on and off, guiding us to the small dirt airstrip next to the church property. The landing was pretty smooth, and as we taxied to a halt, crowds and crowds of people started running next to the plane. Once we had stopped, the crowds surrounded us—hundreds of people! We got out and unloaded the plane, then Matt, a long-term missionary, took me to the stage.

I did a quick setup and we started the meeting at seven. All the others had gone to Mo's house for dinner. I had to wait until after the meeting.

An excerpt from my 2005 journal

At 6:00 P.M. they started. I was the only white person there. The others only started to think about coming when they heard the sound of the music and finally arrived two hours later. I don't think that the sound system is powerful enough; it's difficult maintaining the balance between maximum volume and distortion. . . . I'm so tired. It's hot. I want to go home. I don't think that Africa is the place for me. I just need strength or something. I'm so tired.

This year was not much different! Again, I was the only white person there for a while, and the sound system still wasn't powerful enough—although having a monitor speaker facing us made a huge difference! I loved the conference. There were so many people all dressed so colorfully, all so hungry for the Word—it was just awesome. And the dancers just amazed me—their stamina: one hour of aerobics, twice a day!

> ***An excerpt from my 2005 journal***
> I'm still trying to decide if I should quit my job in England and move here. It's a great opportunity. . . . I'm out of my comfort zone. I want to stay in England; I don't want to be in Africa. BUT, I *do* want to be in Africa! It will be such a difficult life and I don't know if I can handle it. . . .
>
> I think I'm going to say yes. . . .

I am glad I made my decision, although things have been really hard at times. Often, I have just wanted to leave, to go back to a regular job where you are guaranteed a paycheck at the end of each month!

At the conference there were so many people healed, especially deaf people. That just strikes a chord with me. How can you appreciate the beauty of sound when you cannot hear? The smiles on their faces says it ALL.

On Friday night there was so much dust as they were all singing and dancing that some of it got stuck under my contact lens. The next morning I woke up to severe pain and discomfort. My eye was swollen shut, pus was oozing out and it was just nasty. At first I thought that it was conjunctivitis, but then because of the pain I started thinking there was something stuck in there. By this time I couldn't even open my good eye—its movement hurt my other eye, so I was basically blind.

Colleagues rinsed and eye-dropped my eye and covered it with a bandage. I just lay there. It was horrible. Heidi and Rolland were due to speak at a conference in South Africa, so I had actually gone to Malawi to be there specifically for those two days—and there I was, not able to do anything. It made me appreciate my sight so much—and my independence especially.

The conference ended with me having only done five of the eight sessions (still a good ten hours of work per day!), and on Monday morning we loaded up the plane. Two of the visiting preachers were coming back to Pemba with us. They had flown into Blantyre from the States on Wednesday, so we had all their luggage, plus the sound system, plus all our stuff and everything that Heidi had bought at the little airport store!

Rolland carefully weighed each bag and asked each of us our weight. I think we were over the limit the plane could carry. In Nelspruit, the airfield in South Africa where Rolland gets the plane serviced, they call him the Holy Man. It's not because he's involved in missions; it's because he carries loads heavier than any of them dare to. They all think he's crazy!

Before takeoff, Mo drove up and down the runway—his Pinzgauer has a small speaker attached to the roof—announcing in the local dialect, "Clear the runway, remove your cows, chase away the goats and clear the runway!" It was funny. I remember last year, watching as the plane took off, standing next to my father. Never in a thousand years did I expect to be in that plane!

Because my eye was still sore and light sensitive (although getting much better), I sat with it closed for most of the flight. We had to refuel in Blantyre and I managed to clear immigration without my pink eye patch. I wore sunglasses instead!

The flight was quite smooth. Once the plane got its heavy belly off the ground, we were fine. I was feeling airsick, so I closed my eyes and slept.

We were nearing Pemba, and the chatter in the headphones would occasionally wake me up as Charles and Steve chatted to Rolland. Suddenly I woke up and heard, "Oh no, we've lost the vacuum line and gyro compass, and the artificial horizon is gone!" That kind of freaked me out, and one of the passengers asked the

BIG question: "So what does that mean exactly?" Fortunately, it was all okay. Landing would be a bit tricky, but it was all fine.

Another normal day at *Ministério Arco-íris*!

Life principles: Running shoes

God hates the injustice of sickness and wants it to be destroyed. Having watched what God does, now I hate sickness with a passion, too, just as He does. But so often, the battles we win against sickness here are won for others more than ourselves. Several times in my life I have been very sick and I have asked God, "Why is it that I have to fight against sickness?" God said to me, *You are fighting for the Church.* In many ways God is mirroring in my life what He wants to do in the Church. I don't understand why, but He is using me as a kind of prophetic symbol.

In the previous chapter, you read about the life-threatening staph infection that was literally destroying me from the inside out. It was a horrible, agonizing sickness, and yet, God taught me two important lessons through it that I want to pass on to you.

I had been in Malaysia with a friend. I was meant to be looking after her, but I ended up being hospitalized and fed antibiotics through an IV drip. I didn't like being there, so one day I said to her, "Let's just rip the IV out and go and get some Chinese food!" So we did. The hospital staff was not at all happy about this, but we paid my medical bill on the way out, so what could they say?

Soon I returned to Mozambique, still desperately fighting the infection and praying in faith, believing for Jesus' healing. Rolland had been away, and as soon as he returned, he had to board another plane and take me to get specialist care in a hospital in South Africa. I was raging with fever and burning up with pain. I could barely stand up and I was in agony.

In South Africa I learned the first lesson, an important principle for all who want to move in a healing anointing and also for those who want to experience God's healing in their own lives:

thankfulness and rejoicing. Often when we are prayed for, we feel a little better but maybe are aware that we are not *fully* healed. We always tend to look for instantaneous, complete healing, instead of rejoicing in the fact that God has touched us. In that hospital I learned to give thanks for every little bit of healing God gave as He gave it.

I became grateful for every little step I could take until I was able to run and jump. With every step I took, I rejoiced in what Jesus was doing. I didn't moan and say, "But I can only take a few little steps. . . ." Rejoicing is so important.

The second lesson I learned was that God made me to run my course and finish my race. I learned that you must never take your eyes off the finish line and never give in. So even in my sickness I was determined to run—both physically and spiritually.

On my first day in the hospital, I said to Rolland, "Oh no, I forgot to bring my running shoes." It was a stupid statement in the face of my sickness. Just walking a few paces was agonizing. Nevertheless, I told Rolland, "I forgot my running shoes. Go and get some!" Rolland didn't argue with me. He just said, "Okay," and went off to a shopping mall and found me some running shoes. He didn't come back with a bunch of flowers and say to me, "Look, you really won't be running, so I brought these." Neither did he say, "Woe is me, my sick wife is dying." He just brought back what I asked for. He knew I was determined not to die. Rather, I was determined to run!

While I was in the hospital, Jesus took the opportunity to reach out to the spiritually malnourished around me. One doctor came to me and told me that I'd better think about writing my epitaph! Not very good bedside manners, but God bless him anyway. I bought him a Bible. He was a Russian doctor who had never read or even seen one before. I talked to him about Jesus, and the presence of God filled my room.

As time went on, God's presence got thicker and thicker in my room, until eventually the ladies who came in to change my sheets wouldn't leave. They wanted to stay in my room, and they just kept weeping. Often at 4:00 A.M. I would find myself praying for hospital staff members because there was a constant line of them continually coming to my room. They would say to me, "There's so much life in this room!"

After 32 days of battling, tired and weary, I prayed, "God, I know Your presence can kill this staph infection. Your presence can kill what antibiotics cannot. You are a powerful God who destroys the work of the enemy." I was determined to see the power of God manifest in my little jar of clay. It was then that Rolland and I decided we would leave the hospital and go to visit another "Specialist." We decided we would, after all, attend a conference in Toronto I was due to speak at. It was while I was there preaching, clutching the lectern, hardly able to stand, that our Sovereign Lord healed me completely and I danced in His presence once again!

Just like an insidious staph infection that eats away at you from the inside out, the enemy wants to eat away at the Body of Christ. He wants to destroy what God wants to make beautiful and glorious. The Church has been slow to run, so slow to move. But the Lord wants to heal our bones, our ligaments and our joints, and cause us to run the race and finish what He has set before us.

Never reduce your theology to your experience! Believe every word that God says. Be thankful for everything. And know that it is time to get out your running shoes and finish your race. Run with perseverance and never, ever give up!

Chapter 8

Christmas in Revival

December 2005–January 2006

Update from Rolland and Heidi
News archive: posted December 26, 2005

I [Rolland] can hear the waves of the Indian Ocean softly wash up on the rocks and coral of Pemba's beach out in the dark. The air is warm and still. All is peaceful at our funky, thatched house far to the north in Mozambique. And it is 3:00 A.M., time to rise. I have more than a thousand miles to travel today on a tight schedule. Soon headlights are shining through our gate and the trees. My ride to the airport is here.

I quietly load my baggage into the Land Rover, and we make our way over ruts and sand until we reach the main road and pass by our center. All is quiet and deserted on the streets. We drive up sloping terrain and reach the airport on a hill overlooking Pemba and its huge, pristine bay, which is hardly used. We continue past the tiny terminal building and move out on to the tarmac to our Cessna 206 parked beside a few larger commercial aircraft. My three passengers help me as I load the plane, using a flashlight to see. A security guard wanders over to investigate, but we are okay.

The sky begins to glow and lighten in the east, outlining silvery layers of clouds just above the horizon with orange and red. The control tower is closed, but I had filed my flight plan and paid my fees the night before. Our engine breaks the night silence as it starts, and we taxi out to the runway in a mounting sea breeze. We lift off smoothly and line up on a course that slowly takes us away from the coastline toward the central Mozambican city of Beira, our first stop, four and a half hours to the south.

The rising sun brings brilliance to the canopy of beauty that envelops us. Clouds, exquisitely designed and placed by the Creator, approach us and then flash by with a burst of exhilaration. Hills, rivers and wilderness pass below us. I level off at eight thousand feet and trim for cruise. There is no one to talk to on the radio, so I fill our noise-canceling headsets with rich worship music. . . . On we travel in cozy, smooth comfort, each one of us lost in our own thoughts and prayers.

Once again I am thinking of the Makua, a people group of four million living in remote huts scattered far below us, and how God has so graciously been concentrating His attention on them in the last several years. I dwell on what our Good Shepherd has been doing all over southeast Africa since we arrived in Mozambique over ten years ago. In power and glory He has been finding lost sheep and revealing the Kingdom in ways we never dreamed we would see. All our lives we have pressed toward revival, and now we are overwhelmed with a movement that has grown far beyond our natural ability to watch over.

The harvest field is ripe and ready in Africa. The poor know they need the true and living God, and when they meet Him in Jesus they run to Him. They do not refuse. They are not hardened. They know that finally they have found the desire of their hearts. This Jesus who heals the incurably blind and sick in their villages is eternal love. They want to know more. They want to draw closer. They want pastors, churches and a Bible school now. They can't get enough. They shout, dance, sing and worship with wild energy because Jesus is worthy. They know they cannot overdo their passion for Him. And He responds to them with His Spirit. . . .

Every three months our five Bible schools are filled with new pastors and students from the bush. It is amazing to watch Jesus bring them, more at every session. It is life-changing to watch entire villages come to Jesus as soon as they see His love and power. The Kingdom has indeed come upon us when pagan, syncretistic chiefs grab our microphones and shout to their own people, "This is real! No one could do this but God! Listen to these Christians!"

An insistent, insatiable hunger for the Spirit-filled Christian life and increasing revival is spreading across Africa. Hearing of what the Spirit is doing among us, the desperate are urgently calling us to more countries. Bush conferences are in constant demand. Leaders want input, encouragement, direction and fellowship. The people are starving for God, especially in devastated, war-torn countries. With all the cultural richness of their choirs, robes, rhythm and ways, and the promises of health and wealth they have heard, they know they have nothing without His presence and companionship.

As we fly on, I consider the intensity of the Christmas we just experienced this year, and how it so perfectly illustrates the coming of the Kingdom to the poor of Africa.

A Christmas report

> "When you give a luncheon or dinner, do not invite your friends, your brothers or relatives, or your rich neighbors; if you do, they may invite you back and so you will be repaid. But when you give a banquet, invite the poor, the crippled, the lame, the blind, and you will be blessed. Although they cannot repay you, you will be repaid at the resurrection of the righteous."
>
> Luke 14:12–14

Pouring with sweat and covered with dirt and flies, Heidi and our staff spent five hours one afternoon just before Christmas, bringing the life and joy of the Gospel to the "least of these" in the Maputo city dump near our Zimpeto center. The burning garbage heaps shimmered through smoke and fumes in 113-degree heat, but nothing stopped all the celebration. We distributed sacks of food to everyone. Ladies wrapped in their colorful skirts danced with joy. Choirs sang with amazing beauty and harmony. We offered communion with bread and water—all we had in this poor community—to believers. When we finished with the expected number, we still had more toys in our boxes, and so we opened up the queue again for latecomers! Because Jesus died, there is always enough. . . .

Back up north in Pemba, we began our Christmas Eve with a beautiful dinner for our staff near the beach in the warm night air under brilliant stars. We are amazed and grateful for the quality of our many Iris family leaders, both foreign and Mozambican, whom Jesus has given us for His work. Their love, faith and dedication have made us so rich and full. We did not have snow and a roaring fireplace, but our time together was filled with warmth and joy.

Then, late into the night, we began our midnight candlelight service for all our children and workers. With our kids running, jumping and shouting with burning candles mounted on paper plates in the dark, it was holy chaos rather than silent night. But in the warm, flickering glow and dancing shadows, we also sang and worshiped on our faces before our King. We had lights and decorations, and even a gorgeously lit tree, but Jesus was the burning attraction in our hearts. What an amazing time and atmosphere it was, considering that three years ago we began in Pemba with no facilities and just fifteen believers in this "unreachable" town. Finally, we fell into bed at 3:00 A.M. . . .

» p. 110 » p. 111

Christmas Day was packed with joyful activity. We invited our Moslem friends and the media to our new center that we are developing. Our several hundred children had just moved to their new dorm rooms and could hardly be more excited. Heidi and our staff began by passing out gift bags of presents, beginning with the youngest little girls (see photos). Our missionaries had made a tremendous effort to buy these presents and get them to Pemba, and it was priceless to watch neglected, abandoned and orphaned children receive gifts for the first time in their lives. They hardly knew how to react, but we knew they had come to feel loved and valued at last.

Next, we held a Christmas service in our huge green-and-white-striped meeting tent. It was hot, another summer day in blowing dust, but the Holy Spirit had come to Pemba. The gentle breeze of Jesus blew refreshingly over pastors, children and visitors as we married Carlos, one of our Bible school teachers, and his bride, a full orphan from Dondo. What a beautiful time for a wedding, Mozambican style! We are grateful for those who have given rings and wedding gowns to Iris so we can bless many poor couples who want to be married by us.

Of course, we also preached and gave an altar call, as always. All the children in the community had been invited, and more than one hundred of them came forward for salvation. Then our entire church moved out across the road to the beach, and we baptized hundreds of our new believers in front of a gathering crowd of curious, amazed onlookers. Pemba's people can recognize joy, vitality and good works. Their long-standing resistance to the Gospel is melting as more and more of them wholeheartedly rush into the Savior's arms.

Whitecaps on the horizon decorated our beautiful blue and green water on this unusually windy day. Our children jumped, dived and laughed in the breaking waves as these new creatures in Christ, many of them ex-Moslems, climbed out of the surf, grinning, singing and worshiping, publicly identifying with the supernatural life of Jesus.

Adding to the excitement, a visitor and well-known horse trainer from England introduced a sleek, beautiful thoroughbred horse she had brought to Pemba for the children to enjoy. She rode up and down the beach, even taking the horse deep into the water, as our enthusiastic kids ran behind with a mixture of wonder and cautious fear.

Next, we all walked back to our center for our Christmas feast of chicken, rice, coleslaw and Coca-Cola, a rare and amazing treat for the poor. We called in all we could and finally had a tumultuous gathering of two thousand around our open dining hall filled with Christmas decorations. A group of our young girls energetically performed an African dance they had diligently practiced for the occasion. African drums and dance are always a spine-tingling treat when mixed with the pure joy of the Lord. There were people everywhere, spilled rice and empty Coke bottles all over the floor, scattered benches, paper wrappings—it was wonderful! And the first Christmas most of them had ever experienced.

Heidi was interviewed twice by local radio reporters, with government officials listening. They were amazed by this huge feast given for the poor, including so many outsiders and complete strangers. Heidi spoke of our primary school opening up, offering free education for local children, and our vision for taking in far more children. These Moslem media people were moved, and they are sending a television crew back to cover this new Christian force in their community.

Our fifteen believers of three years ago have grown to more than 240 churches in this province, and more are being added each week. But Jesus wants His whole Makua bride of four million brought in, and so we will press forward with mercy and grace, love and power, until the province has been won, in His beautiful, irresistible way.

Our Iris family enjoyed wonderful Christmas celebrations at our other bases, too. Each reflected the power of the Gospel to bring life and hope to the poor, to any who will receive the Savior. With full hearts we look forward to the best yet in 2006 as we continue to grow in the knowledge of Him. May His life and joy fill the whole continent of Africa!

✣ ✣ ✣

We continue to worship and pray as our little blue-and-white plane slowly moves south through changing skies and weather, clouds and heavy rain, until finally we descend for an instrument approach over Beira's harbor. We have a lot more flying to do before we reach Nelspruit, South Africa, and then I must drive all the way to Johannesburg, leaving my plane in Nelspruit for service. And then I meet and fly out with Heidi on a round-the-world speaking trip, testifying to the Gospel of God's grace. We will never grow weary and lose heart, but we will hope in the Lord, renew our strength and soar on wings like eagles.

Christmas Day in Mozambique

What does Christmas look like at an orphanage with four hundred kids in Mozambique?

[Blog posting from Iris missionary Nancy Anderson, serving at one of the children's homes]

It began on a delightfully cool and cloudy morning with a special breakfast for the kids at 7:00 A.M., including peanut butter on bread and a banana (usually just bread). At 8:00 A.M. in each dorm, each child was given new clothes. Although every dorm is different, it usually means a new shirt, shorts and underwear. Some kids also got socks and sandals. Then "Papa Noel" (Father Christmas), who was three people—the director of the center, the head educator of the kids and the head pastor—went from dorm to dorm to deliver the presents. Every child got a "sack" of some kind, full of things. Most of the bags were decorated and personalized in some way. The bags had everything in them like dolls, lip gloss, nail polish, toy cars, marbles, candy, pens/crayons/markers and paper, twirling tops, little toy pianos, plastic cell phones, plastic balls and Spider-Man toys. The older boys each received a watch, and most dorms had communal dorm gifts like board games, wading pools, books, soccer balls, mini basketball hoops and bikes.

After the gift delivery was church and then a dinner for the community people that involved some chicken on rice (a special meal). The final magical part of the day was the chicken lunch for all the center kids, where they received a quarter chicken, chips, coleslaw, rice and a Coke. You've never seen kids lick the bones clean like this, because they only get a meal like this at Christmas and then at Children's Day on June 1.

What I've just written is more the practical/technical part of what the day looked like. What is much harder to put into words is what it feels like to be here and watch it all happen. Walking into a dorm, I saw sixty-plus kids sitting proudly in new clothes with a look of sheer delight and expectation on their faces as they waited for their gifts. This moved to ecstasy as they opened their bags and, soon after, pandemonium with sixty-plus kids trying out their new things.

I was also delighted to bless a few of my special boys each with his own new soccer ball. One of the boys had tears in his eyes, another had a smile from ear to ear and another gave me a hug I will never forget. For all of these boys, it was the first soccer ball that they've ever been given all to themselves.

My predominant thought all day was that I wouldn't want to be anywhere else on the face of the earth but here. Somehow the looks on each of these kids' faces and the children's appreciation at what little they received taught me the true meaning of Christmas. The truly humbling thought was realizing how much these kids were getting compared to most other children in Mozambique, struggling to survive each day, who would receive nothing.

From Heidi

Posted December 3, 2005 @ 12:00 P.M.

I want to thank you for your amazing response in prayer. While I was in the hospital God spoke to me about His desire for multiplication. I want to see God raise up an entire army of laid-down lovers who will carry His glory to the ends of the earth.

I believe Jesus will release a mass student-volunteer missions movement to help bring the Gospel to every tribe and tongue. A couple of weeks ago, I returned from an intense three-week conference tour during which God spoke to me about ministering to students at Ivy League universities.

We went to Harvard University where the first great revival in America, the Great Awakening, once touched this nation. A young Harvard student named Matteus came up in our meeting and said, "I want to meet the God whom Heidi speaks of, but my mind is too strong." So we prayed for him that his heart would become bigger than his mind! I called for one of the church leaders to come over and hug him. Father God wanted to hug him. Later, I saw Matteus worshiping Jesus passionately, with his hands shaking in the air. He was saying, "I feel God! I feel God! I feel God! He is so strong!"

I felt led to do an altar call for students who felt like orphan children. The Father spoke to me about His heart to heal the youth of America just like He has healed our Mozambican children. Students streamed forward. As soon as we embraced them, the Holy Spirit touched them, and they began to weep. The aisles were full of weeping university students. Some were saved. Many were physically healed. Most of all, Jesus was worshiped yet again in the center of Harvard at Memorial Church!

Rolland and I finally had to leave around 2:00 A.M., since students had to go to class the next morning. As we closed the meeting, students were rolling down the marble stairs of Harvard, overcome by the power of the Holy Spirit. Another leader said to me, "You don't understand. It has probably been decades since anything like this happened at Harvard University!"

God will release this army of obedient missionaries who will not love their lives even unto death. I recall Jim Elliot's famous quote:

> He is no fool who gives what he cannot keep to gain that which he cannot lose.

Now I am thrilled to be home. We just had our yearly regional conference in the south at Zimpeto where hundreds of people were saved. There was a blind boy who had not seen anything for two years. He was instantly healed. His mother was overjoyed. The Lord spoke to me that there were ten women in the meeting who had severe back pain because of issues of unforgiveness. As soon as they came forward and repented, Jesus healed all ten. I also heard from the Lord that there was a deaf man there. I had to wait thirty minutes for him to come forward. (I guess someone had to tell him what I had said!) He was healed and told me that Jesus brought him to the meeting. Worthy is the Lamb!

We went to our base in Dondo for another conference, and God showed up in an extraordinary way. I was calling on the Holy Spirit to move upon the people when He came like a whirlwind. People began to twirl around and fall to the ground. That night, more than we could count were healed. At the end of the last evening meeting, I hopped in the back of our pickup truck to get home, and some of our boys ran up to ask me to pray for a new youth living at our center. He was blind. The presence of God came upon him, and he was healed. The youth were blessed beyond belief.

» p. 111 » p. 112 » p. 112

I had the best homecoming of all when I reached Pemba. The children were all at the airport, singing and rejoicing with me for my miraculous healing. They had prayed and fasted for days, believing for this miracle. What an awesome family we have. On outreach this week, hundreds were saved! I so enjoyed praying for a young boy born deaf whose ears opened up. His father was beside himself with joy!

You are precious to me. Thank you again for praying for me and for remembering the poor!

Much love in Jesus,
Heidi

Responses to blog posting

Cathy VS: December 9, 2005 @ 5:21 P.M.

God is causing me to lay down my life more and more for Him, and I know I long to be part of that student-volunteers mission. My life is being lost more and more in Jesus. Every day I fall more in love with Him. I love Africa and seeing what God is doing in and around His people there.

Kimberly S: December 14, 2005 @ 5:32 A.M.

Heidi, did you know that on the day your report was posted, a report from Paul Strand of CBN was also posted, entitled "Revival Predicted to Shake New England"? He also recently wrote about spiritual awakening on Ivy League campuses.

Sid C: December 16, 2005 @ 8:36 P.M.

Thank You, God, for what You have done at Harvard. We need You to do the same in our universities in England, God. Please remember the U.K. We are hungry and thirsty for God to break out here.

Thanks from Rolland

We were deeply moved by the overwhelming outpouring of love and prayer that we received from all over the world when Heidi was dangerously sick and in the hospital for a month. Finally, at just the right time, Jesus healed her in a matter of minutes while preaching a message of grace and joy in the face of all satanic opposition.

It is our joy to receive fresh opportunity every day to live out the Sermon on the Mount in the power of the Spirit. We glory in our weaknesses, for then we are strong. We lose our lives for His sake and yet we cannot lose, but instead we become more than conquerors. We want always to live for the praise of His glory. Please keep interceding for us!

A Christmas report photos

1. Our midnight candlelight service on Christmas Eve

2. Wonder and curiosity over Christmas presents

From Heidi photos

1. Cooking for the conference at Dondo

2. Our children in church at Zimpeto in the south

3. Our family of boys with Heidi and Dr. Guy Chevreau at our new center

Chapter 9

Our Job Is to Love

February–March 2006

Heidi's blog entry

Posted February 25, 2006 @ 2:18 P.M.

» p. 122 » p. 122 » p. 123 » p. 123

I had a wild and wonderful January on an eleven-country tour. My favorite spot was among the Bulgarian gypsies with our friends Georgian and Winnie Banov. There are so many stories of God pouring out His love. One that shows the love of the Father for the sick comes to mind. A mother brought to me her son who was nearly blind. He saw only fuzzy gray shadows. As I held him in my arms for quite a while, he began to cry. He could see absolutely everything clearly for the first time in his life. The three of us embraced and wept together, thanking Jesus for what He had just done. It was a tremendous joy to see the fruit of the Banovs' labor of love poured out among the poor for so many years. I felt at home among these people.

I have been back in Pemba for a while, though it seems like more has happened in a few days than in the previous year! Miracles are on the increase. Thursday night, when we went to a village in the "bush bush"[3] of Cabo Delgado, I called the deaf to come forward after hundreds of people were saved. Finally Tanya, one of our missionaries, brought to the children and me a deaf boy who was instantly healed. After his mother testified, five more deaf people were brought to me, including a deaf-mute totally out of her mind. Together the children and I laid our hands upon each one. Jesus mercifully and kindly healed them all. The deaf-mute was also able to speak as she was restored to her right mind. The Kingdom of God belongs to the children! The village surely is being turned upside down by the love of God. We will be building a church in this very village next week.

At our Pemba base, as hundreds of pastors and Bible students gather in the dirt, raggedly clothed and often without shoes, the sweet Holy Spirit comes in day after day and causes transformation in the lives of the poor. They eagerly study the Word and long to see their provinces transformed. They have taught me what true riches are. The Kingdom belongs to the poor in spirit.

Along with all our blessings, we have also gone through some severe trials, too numerous to tell. Please remember to pray for us. One of our workers tried to murder another of our workers. It has been very traumatic. Also this week, the government was initially very antagonistic toward our first primary school in the province of Cabo Delgado. But after prayer and fasting, we seem to be getting some kind of breakthrough. We are adding children to our numbers almost daily. They continue to delight our hearts.

Remember to stop for the one.

Much love in Jesus,
Heidi

[3] "Bush bush"—Heidi's term to describe an out-of-the-way part of what many would already consider to be a very remote area.

From Georgian Banov
[http://www.riverlution.net/january06bulgaria.htm]

Our personal highlight and joy this month was introducing Rolland and Heidi Baker of Iris Ministries to our beloved gypsies in Bulgaria for the first time. It was the coldest winter in one hundred years, and our building did not have any heat. We had to keep dancing to keep warm!

Amazingly, the gypsies came in droves in spite of the cold; they were so hungry for more of God. Instant healings were popping like popcorn, and the Bakers left behind a rich deposit for healing in the revival soil there. Rolland and Heidi were perfectly at home among the gypsies, as their hearts are filled with love and compassion for the poorest of the poor.

Letter from Heidi
Posted March 25, 2006 @ 12:40 A.M.

Thank you so much for keeping in touch and praying for me. It really helps us to know that we are covered in prayer, especially when things get difficult. One of our beautiful babies, whom I named Maria Esperanza, died last night. She was a gift, a treasure loaned to us for a short time. We all miss her.

Recently, I've been undone by 1 John 4:7–8 and 16 (NASB):

> Beloved, let us love one another, for love is from God; and everyone who loves is born of God and knows God. The one who does not love does not know God, for God is love. . . . We have come to know and have believed the love which God has for us. God is love, and the one who abides in love abides in God, and God abides in him.

I have one goal: to be found inside His love.

The Lord has been reminding me that our job is to love. I want to keep it simple. I could tell you about the thousands of churches and the mighty revival that is taking place. I could tell you about the thousands of people we are feeding every day. I could tell you about all the signs, wonders and miracles. But I prefer to tell you about one life, a little boy named Selsun. This Friday I found him wandering the streets of Maputo, sad, despondent and rejected. I walked in the back streets with him, making friends. I went to where he was living, under a veranda. I found out his parents died in a train crash and his aunt beat him. She did not want him. I was reminded that it is all about loving the one in front of us. We decided to take him to our Zimpeto center. Hanna, one of our missionaries, will be taking care of him. He now loves Jesus. He has a home. He is no longer afraid or alone. Now he can see his dreams fulfilled and go to school! We need to keep it simple and love the one in front of us. Thank you for caring. You are loved.

Much love in Jesus,
Heidi

Responses to blog posting
Julie: March 30, 2006 @ 6:50 P.M.

Whenever I want to be transported deep inside the Father's heart, I visit this site and instantly I am there. It's all about You, Jesus; it's all about love. I can't help but see and feel the same things over and over again when I look at the pictures of these precious children of His. God's heart is made up of what they resemble—humility. God is love.

Giana S: April 6, 2006 @ 4:44 P.M.

I am heartbroken at the great love of our Father, that in His Son we can experience His love, kindness, goodness and blessings. He is so good. I am so hungry and thirsty for God.

Ben M: April 19, 2006 @ 8:59 P.M.

Dear Heidi,
I am seven years old. I have been learning about missionaries. Thank you for what you are doing for God's children. I will be praying for you.

Your friend,
Ben

To see what God sees

Joanna Morrison: posted March 31, 2006 @ 10:14 P.M.

How do we gain the right perspective in the midst of such hopelessness, fear, hunger and devastation? In the same way as the prophets before us, who, confused by the devastation around them, withdrew into the "presence of the Lord." There they would begin to see with eyes of faith the hearts longing for love, the Church being transformed into a perfect Bride, the individuals God had brought into their lives for a touch of His great love.

While I know this is the right perspective, I often feel the desperation of not having anything to give because I have failed to enter the presence of the Lord. God is always gracious, always reaching out to welcome me into His arms. Sometimes He speaks to me in spite of my wrong perspective, and for that I give thanks.

We had been talking about hosting a women's conference in Bangula for some months. All of a sudden in early February we saw that the time was now. The women had finished hoeing and planting and therefore had time to come. They were waiting for rain, and they were suffering hunger. It seemed a good time to gather together and draw encouragement from each other and from the Word.

I was nervous, as I always am when a large group gathers. The pressing bodies, the sickness, the complaining, the strong smells of urine and sweat, all make me want to run. I confessed my fear to the commissioners' wives, whom I meet with every week, and asked them to pray for me.

Before every meeting, I walked around our church building, greeting the women. They love to hear me speak Chichewa. Many asked me to pray, and so my walk to greet turned into a walk to pray. I prayed and prayed and prayed, for children with terribly sticky eyes, for legs shriveled up because of years of heavy labor, for congested chests and deep coughs. I called out to God not to let the women miss out because they were sick and distracted. I prayed for His Kingdom to come. I called the women to come and worship. They gathered together, and I tried to play their worship songs on my flute but was soon lost. We sang for at least an hour and everyone danced. I got out some flags I had made, and several women grasped them eagerly.

I spoke from John 6 and Luke 14. God seemed to tie them together for me—the invitation to a banquet and the feast being the body and blood of Jesus. The first night I spoke in Chichewa, as there was no translator present. I told the story of Jesus feeding the five thousand and said that Jesus *sees* our need and *knows* what He is going to do. All that is required of us is *faith*, small or big, that God can do anything. Though Jesus sees us and knows what is needed, He still invites us to this feast. It is our choice. In the parable of the banquet, all the invited guests had excuses. Still, in the end, the house was filled with the poor and the needy. Will you come to the feast? Jesus invites you. The feast that Jesus invites you to answers a hunger that is far deeper than the hunger for food that so often drives us. He wants to satisfy the hunger in each of us to know God. He wants to feed us His body and His blood. What does that mean? Well, Jesus did not consider His body too important to lay it down, His blood too important to shed for us. If we are to take up His life, it will be at the expense of our own.

A surprise came to me as I spoke. I realized that these words about "counting the cost" spoke directly into the overly dependent Malawian family. The family ties are so strong, be it a brother in trouble or a disappointed mother-in-law, and no one wants to let go. Can you love Jesus more than your mother? More than your father? More than your own life? That's how much He wants. Can you release your children to love Jesus more than they love you? That's what He wants.

In Malawi, there is a very common sight—the unfinished house. Many people begin to build and then run out of money. Jesus' story about this challenges us to count the cost ahead of time. Taking up the life of Jesus could be costly. It will be a life of humility, suffering, leaving behind, but, at the same time, a life of joy, an abundant life. Jesus, for the joy set before Him, endured the cross [see Hebrews 12:2]. Our joy is with Jesus. The party begins today as we take up the life of Christ, but the focus is heaven. We will worship the Lamb, and He will wipe away our tears and lead us to living water. The sun will no longer burn, and there will be no more hunger. Hallelujah!

As our churches are spread out all over Malawi, we have not visited all of them. The task seems too big, but we must remember that Christ is the head of the Church and He will not leave them, no matter how small or remote the village. There is a lot of poor, if not wrong, teaching in Malawian churches. In time we hope to train up all of our pastors so that they can at least get some things right. In the meantime we trust God completely. He is the Great Shepherd, whose sheep follow Him because they know His voice.

Life principles: How deep?

God loves us so much that He wants to destroy our preconceptions about Him, so that His Holy Spirit can move freely among us. God likes to shatter the boxes we create in order to contain Him and His work among us. The fact is, God does not like being put in a box! God is sovereign and holy. He likes to be God! He wants us to participate in His divine nature, follow in His footsteps. But He makes all the decisions. We just follow. God likes to be in control. He wants to take over because that is just God doing His thing. Our job is to be yielded lovers, willing to cooperate with Him.

A few years ago I determined that I didn't care how God used me; I just wanted to be fully possessed by His Holy Spirit. That is my prayer every day. Consequently, I often don't know what day it is, what time it is, what country I'm in or what time my flight is leaving! My only desire is to be led by the Spirit wherever and whenever. I just hope somebody puts me on my plane when I'm due to be on it! I often don't know where I am going, but I do know that I'm in love. That's all that matters to me.

In Ezekiel 47, Ezekiel is given a prophetic vision by God. The angel of the Lord leads him deeper and deeper into the river that flows from the temple of God. What is this "river of God" that is talked about so much? When we speak of the river of God, we are talking about Jesus, about His manifest glory. The river is not an "it"; it is a "Him." God draws us into the river so that we can be immersed in Him. He desires to swallow us up until we are not seen anymore. We must allow ourselves to be so immersed in His presence that He has total control over us; until His glory-presence enfolds us in such a way that we start thinking His thoughts, until His heart begins to beat inside us and we feel its rhythm.

The angel of the Lord was asking Ezekiel, in effect, "How deep do you want to get?" How deep into the heart of God are you willing to go? How deep into His presence do you want to be? God wants to saturate you in His presence—to literally drown you! Yes, God wants you dead! But then He will kiss you to life, a new creation, to be the fragrance of Christ to a dying world.

At first Ezekiel only went into the water up to his ankles. Most of us like the thought of that. When we are ankle-deep in God, it feels good, because we can still do our thing. We've got something of God, but we can walk and talk and, more importantly, be in control.

The angel of the Lord said to Ezekiel, as God says to us today, "I want you to come in deeper than that." God wants us to lose ourselves in Him, to be out of our depth in His presence, carried away by the irresistible currents of His love. God is wooing us, persuading us to go deeper and deeper into Him. He is leading us into the glory-presence of the Most High, into a place where we will no longer be in control, but rather out of control, fully yielded to His Spirit.

In Mozambique we live in two locations, one of which is by the ocean. Every day when I am praying, I love to be by the water. Often I love to snorkel, mainly because nobody can get me when I'm underwater! In the water is my favorite place to pray (second only to prayer-walking in foreign countries where nobody knows me). I love to be alone with God. I get agitated if I don't get that time alone with Him, because He is my breath, my life, my power, my love. He is my everything, and I cannot function without Him. Ezekiel waded out until he was knee-deep in the water, and when you are knee-deep, you begin to feel the current. But knee-deep is still too safe. I am into being fully immersed. God's aim for you is to have you live "underwater," so deeply immersed in Him that you no longer think like a "normal" person but are totally consumed with Him.

Perhaps God has spoken to you about what He sees for your life, and yet you are still only knee-deep in the water, at best. You will never come into the fullness of your destiny until you allow God to draw you in and drag you under. You have to die first! Then you will see God's purpose for your life come to pass. He will resurrect you, so you need not be afraid, only surrender completely to Him.

How deep will you go into Him? Wade out into the waters of His presence, and whatever you do, don't stop until you are completely submerged in His love, mercy and grace.

Heidi's blog entry photos

1. A record cold winter in a Bulgarian gypsy neighborhood with Georgian and Winnie Banov

2. Georgian and his violin with Bulgarian gypsies in passionate, united celebration

3. Gypsies at the altar with Heidi in a freezing cold hall

4. Affectionate, abandoned gypsy worship

Chapter 10

African Diamonds in the Making

April–May 2006

Heidi's blog entry

Posted May 17, 2006 @ 7:55 P.M.

One Sunday in Pemba

» p. 141 » p. 141 » p. 142 » p. 142

Sunday was a beautiful day. Church was filled with singing, dancing Makua and Macondie friends, along with many visitors from around the world. I preached from Mark 16:15–18:

> He said to them, "Go into all the world and preach the good news to all creation. Whoever believes and is baptized will be saved, but whoever does not believe will be condemned. And these signs will accompany those who believe: In my name they will drive out demons; they will speak in new tongues; they will pick up

> snakes with their hands; and when they drink deadly poison, it will not hurt them at all; they will place their hands on sick people, and they will get well."

In Mozambique we see King Jesus protect us from great opposition as He promised in this passage. During church, several people gave their testimonies. One lady had been full of demons and was told by her witch doctor to eat her family! She was severely sick and could not sleep. She would cut her arm and drink her own blood. When she came to church, I would hug her and pray she would know the love of Jesus. Then one of our pastors visited her and burned all her witch doctor fetishes, and almost immediately she was freed and filled with the peace of Jesus. This morning her face was beaming with love, and instead of eating her family members, she has become their friend!

The next lady had an even more amazing story testifying to God's grace and power to protect us all. She had been very ill with acute asthma for ten years. Her husband was sure she was a prostitute and was going to divorce her. Recently, she came to our church in Pemba, as demonized as anyone we have seen. She was healed of asthma and set free instantly by prayer and a hug filled with the love of Jesus. Her husband was amazed by her transformation, although he continued to drink and fly into crazy rages. One day he had a demonic fit and died. After he was pronounced dead at the hospital, his wife began to pray in Jesus' name. In a little over an hour he was raised from the dead—and came straight to the church to ask Jesus into his heart! At the same time he was set free from the demons who had tormented him for years. This morning he announced with a huge smile that he has not had a drink of alcohol since that day.

Right after I preached on this passage, we went across the street and were baptizing new converts and many of our new children. What a joy to see the sunlight on their shining faces! As they were baptized in the turquoise water, they were filled with the presence of the glorious Lamb who was slain. Church lasted until three in the afternoon! What a beautiful Sunday in Pemba. This is what I was created for.

Thank you for loving and praying for us. Thank you for remembering the poor.

Much love in Jesus,
Heidi

Response to blog posting
Lex W: May 28, 2006 @ 10:44 P.M.

I pray for the day when such miraculous demonstrations of the power of Jesus will follow all those who believe across the world. After all, that's what we are called to do!

Update from Rolland and Heidi
News archive: posted May 29, 2006

The sparkling edges of the Indian Ocean are rippling gently on the rocky sand before me at low tide here in Pemba. The brilliant noon sun is accenting ribbons of green, turquoise and blue tropical water with intense flashes of reflected light that add dazzle to the shimmering surface. The restful sound of surf is mingling with the rustling of shade trees that form a rich green canopy over our yard and simple, funky house. From my table on our roof under some African thatch, I look out over grass and flowers at this wide vista of clear, warm, ever-moving water that is Mozambique's coast—one of the world's last untouched environmental treasures.

I am looking at the glory of the Creator who does all things well. His workmanship is superb, in nature and in us. He knows how to glorify Himself and to protect His honor and reputation in this world. His will is spectacular, joyous and beyond improvement. His Kingdom is the home of righteousness and perfection. His purposes will be accomplished on the earth. He is thrilled with the progress of His Church and where she is going. The dust, chaff and residual sin of this world do not bring Him down. He is not discouraged and at a loss. He is not just hoping for better things from us, but He is powerfully at work in us, and He will succeed!

Our enemy will use every possible device to convince us otherwise. We will give him less attention and Jesus our Savior more. We will concentrate not on weaknesses in ourselves and dark forces of danger on all sides, but on His face. We are sustained by beholding His beauty. We are confident in His cross. We are satisfied by what He has done. His Gospel is all-sufficient. We will immerse ourselves forever in the river that flows from His throne. We are more than conquerors through Him who loved us!

We choose His perspective. From another perspective, Heidi and I, along with our whole ministry, have been assaulted relentlessly these four months since our last newsletter. We are exhausted, overextended and overrun by needs, crises, corruption, disappointment and the desperate cry for relief that rises up constantly from the poor of the world. And we cannot keep up with the demand for spiritual relief that calls for our attention from all over the world.

But His mercies and compassions never fail; they are new every morning. We are never discouraged, for "we have this treasure in jars of clay to show that this all-surpassing power is from God and not from us. We are hard pressed on every side, but not crushed; perplexed, but not in despair; persecuted, but not abandoned; struck down, but not destroyed. We always carry around in our body the death of Jesus, so that the life of Jesus may also be revealed in our body" (2 Corinthians 4:7–10).

Here in Africa, among the poorest of the poor, we are seeing revival fueled and sustained by the power of God, in spite of all our weaknesses. Onlookers react in all different ways, and there is always so much to criticize, but at the core of this movement is a white-hot, total abandonment to Jesus and His Kingdom. We will not be led astray from the simplicity and purity of devotion to Him. We are advancing. Our weapons are a firm faith, gentleness, peace, patience and a love that cannot be resisted. In Him we cannot lose!

Since January Heidi and I have been preaching our hearts out. Between us this year we have been to Canada, Australia, Eastern Europe, Taiwan, the east and west coasts of America, Korea, Brazil, England and Sudan. Now Heidi is heading for France as I go to Singapore. But what we preach is most intensely tested and refined in the fires of poverty and suffering in Africa. We descend into the darkness and find that Jesus is there, in glory and power, and that He is a perfect Savior for any who want Him. Through the humble and poor of Africa, He calls the rich and powerful to Himself, winning hearts around the world with His matchless ways.

Though we travel outside Africa a third of the year and minister in many countries in Africa, we continue to concentrate on Pemba and the northern province of Cabo Delgado in Mozambique. Our second Holy Given missions school starts there next week, when students from twelve nations will arrive to learn missions on the mission field by listening, studying, worshiping, getting "wrecked" by the Holy Spirit, serving and ministering among the poor daily for ten weeks. Our base in Pemba is becoming an intense hub of activity where we care for hundreds of children, operate a free primary school for the community, train pastors in our Bible school and launch outreaches out across the province where more than three hundred churches have been planted in three years. The "unreachable" Makua people group around us is coming to Jesus, village by village, night by night.

The Holy Spirit's pattern among us continues. . . . As remote villages have been responding to the Gospel week after week all this year, our meetings in our big tent at our Pemba center have been filled more and more with the glory of the Lord. We shout and dance up a storm as only Africans can, in the dirt and heat with clouds of dust rising from stomping feet. Pastors, missionaries, children and visitors together get lost in passionate, fiery celebration. But then the dust settles as a hush comes over us. The Holy Spirit quiets our hearts in perfect peace, and we transition into worship, deep and powerful. Then something amazing happens—the children begin to lead. They gather to sing to their Savior, and their soft, clear, gentle voices blend and harmonize with holy artistry, thrilling and spine tingling. The Holy Spirit has come to rest among us and find His dwelling place.

At such times God has been giving some of our pastors and children heavenly visitations and visions. One Friday during chapel, our twelve-year-old Crispen was worshiping the Lord. Suddenly, he had a clear vision of something very dark flying out of his heart. He saw a brilliant white light come into his heart and explode. Then he heard a voice that said, *We are more than conquerors!* He came to Heidi and asked if she knew what it meant. He was undone by the Holy Spirit. Then one Monday morning during worship, one of our student pastors, Fernando, had an amazing vision. He saw the powerful hand of God pick him up and place him in a cemetery in the middle of dry bones. The Lord told him to preach to the bones and tell them they had new life in Christ Jesus. He was very afraid, but God told him not to fear because He was with him. So he preached to the bones and they became living people. . . .

From the freezing cold gypsy huts of eastern Bulgaria to the 115-degree heat of Sudanese refugee camps, from the isolated native Inuits of arctic Canada to the dirt-poor subsistence farmers along the Zambezi River, we see a ravenous desire for God among the poor and lowly. We will preach with all our strength to those who will listen, those who will receive, those who know they need Him. Jesus knows their suffering, and He will make it up to them. He will be their God, and they will be His people. He will use them to shame the wise and make the world jealous of their wealth toward Him.

» p. 143

It is a privilege beyond price to see the joy and affection of the Holy Spirit poured out like a waterfall on people who have known so much severe hardship, disappointment and bitter loneliness in their lives. Jesus is the perfect Redeemer, and it is a wonder to watch how He works, where He chooses to reveal Himself and on whom His Spirit comes to rest. We crave being at the center of the vortex of His activity in this world, missing nothing. We will go anywhere and do anything if only we can participate in His most transcendent, breathtakingly irresistible work.

In this process we also encounter the worst Satan can do. Our enemies in Pemba try to get us deported. They publicly slander our motives and threaten us with lawsuits and prison. They falsify charges, demand restitution for crimes we didn't commit, threaten our staff with murder, waste and steal our money and strike for whatever they choose. Ministry to the poor involves vastly more than becoming a provider of food and clothes. It means much more than healing bodies and generating wealth. Bringing the Kingdom means a supernatural kindling of that most fundamental quality of revival—a hunger and thirst for righteousness. It means a thundering cataract of mercy and grace that cuts through the hard rock of evil like Niagara Falls with clean, refreshing purity, blowing like wet mist in the gentle breeze of Jesus. Africa is rich with diamonds buried deep in the ground, but one by one God is transforming the poor of Africa into sparkling diamonds in the Spirit, perfect and marvelous for all to see.

For this we will die. For this we will lose our lives for His sake. For this we will give up all, take up our cross and follow Him. We are enthralled and energized by all that fires the heart of God Himself. He remembers every tear. He repays us. And we will share His life and glory.

Pray for us always, that we will not falter and fail here in Africa. Join us in our work as you are gifted and empowered by Him. May our closeness in Him result in great fruit that will last. May righteousness, peace and joy rule our lives as His signs and wonders confirm our message and follow us everywhere. May Jesus Himself be with you richly in return for your amazing, faithful support all these months. May you comprehend what you are contending for with us and may we together enter into the joy of our Master.

Much love in Jesus,
Rolland and Heidi

Rolland's blog entry

Posted May 31, 2006 @ 6:17 P.M.

Situation for Iris in Pemba

I'm in a conference in a town in Gaza Province in southern Mozambique while Heidi is in Pemba. I just got a call from her about a very serious situation for Iris that erupted today in Pemba.

As you may imagine, Moslem leaders and the more Marxist and antiforeign elements in Mozambique are very agitated about our growth and influence in this country. Such leaders in Pemba have actually expressed their outrage at Iris when they cannot even prevent their own children from coming to church and getting filled with the Spirit.

You may remember how we were evicted from our center in 1997 by Marxists and had everything taken from us. Something similar is being attempted now in Pemba.

Today, a major story appeared on the front page of Pemba's newspaper, apparently instigated by people anxious for our removal from Mozambique. It was blatantly reported for the whole city to read that, among many other things, we are using North American religion to subvert the government; that we are anti-Frelimo (the political party now in power); that all our contacts with leaders are designed to undermine the party; that we're anti-black and anti-Africa, etc.

Heidi has spent ten years becoming Mozambican in heart and soul and has a permanent Mozambican visa. Everything she does is for "her" country, Mozambique. But the article is describing her as deceptive and treacherous. She feels so attacked and devastated. The threat is real. Last year the government very nearly tore down our center with its buildings at our expense.

We are meeting with the editor and want to write an article in response together with a Mozambican lawyer. Meanwhile, we are asking you, our friends, to have your networks pray for us. This is yet another critical hour.

On we go in Jesus,
Much love,
Rolland and Heidi

Responses to blog posting
Tom G: June 2, 2006 @ 12:59 A.M.

Just translated that into German and put it on my blog. German readers of my blog will stand with you in Christ's victory against this.

Carol DL: June 2, 2006 @ 8:24 A.M.

We are believing that our Lord will complete what He has begun. Praise God that we can join you in this, and around the world, prayers are going up. We give God the glory in all that He will do, in Jesus' name.

Heather N: June 2, 2006 @ 8:11 P.M.

I am praying that the Lord will be a ring of fire around you and the glory in the midst of you! May the Father give you His keys to the government of Mozambique, and may His light and truth burst forth in the midst of the darkness.

Blog update

[Teisa Miller, Iris missionary]

Posted April 26, 2006 @ 8:20 A.M.

What a blessing it is to know and share the love of Jesus Christ! This month I want to share another love lesson from above.

On the same day I sent my sappy Valentine's email to everyone, unknown to us a young pregnant teenage girl and her mother were in danger of being forced to leave a local hospital. The young girl had been extremely sick for months, and now it was time to give birth. The hospital staff considered refusing to help her because she had no money and would most likely die. Upon hearing about the situation, Dr. Carlos (a Cuban doctor and Iris volunteer) offered to deliver the baby by caesarean. A precious four-pound baby girl was born.

The next day, the baby's mother died in the hospital due to an internal infection. After hearing about Iris Ministries from Dr. Carlos, the grandmother wrapped the tiny, one-day-old baby in her *capalona* (Mozambican skirt) and started to walk to our center. It must have taken her four hours in the hot, African sun.

The grandmother explained to our staff that she was also sick and that she could not care for the baby. The dear lady shared how she didn't have any milk; she kept pulling out her withered breast to prove it. Within twenty minutes the paperwork was signed, the grandmother said good-bye and we added another amazing treasure to our family. Our staff took the baby girl to Heidi's office. After praying for her, Heidi named her Maria Esperanca [*esperanca* is Portuguese for "hope"].

Many of us continually fussed over Maria: where she would sleep overnight, who got to give her a bath, who got to have her for the day, etc. Em (the head missionary over babies) had her most nights, but when her roommate came down with a cold, we decided Maria would stay with me for the week. Wow! I cannot express the beauty of loving and caring for Maria. In the physical,

God was using her to reveal the glory and sacrifice of motherhood to me. In the Spirit, God was using Maria to reveal the wonder of love, His limitless love, in which we move, live and have our being. We have been miraculously chosen to be His hands, His voice, His heart to a lost and dying world. Maria made His call to love so candidly clear and tangible.

And then Maria got sick. We laid hands on her and prayed. Later that night we took her to the local hospital. Things seemed to get a bit better the next day, but the hospital would not let anyone see her because she was in the isolation room on oxygen. But we still went to see her, loving her through the window and praying for her in the hall.

The following day, Jesus took our precious Maria to heaven. Manela, the educator, was at the hospital when she died. She came back to the center and pulled Em out of home group. Then Rabia and another missionary left. When I saw them comforting Em and Manela, it hit me. Someone made the announcement about what had happened. We as a family cried and prayed together.

The next day the hospital refused to let us have her body. There is a horrible law here about babies not being recognized as citizens until they are one year old. In Mozambique, where death is so tragically normal (one out of five babies dies within twelve months), babies are buried in daily mass graves. We still gathered for a short prayer service on the day she would have been one month old.

When I came in January of 2005 we had 80 kids. We now have 172 and are still growing. For an entire year and a half, we did not lose one child to sickness or accident—until Maria. For a few days, I had no peace. I could not understand why God gave us Maria, only to take her away so quickly. In painful sincerity, I expressed my confusion, questions and doubts to God, not so much in words, but more in tears.

> Record my lament;
> list my tears on your scroll—
> are they not in your record?

Then my enemies will turn back
  when I call for help.
  By this I will know that God is for me.
In God, whose word I praise,
  in the LORD, whose word I praise—
in God I trust. . . .

Psalm 56:8–11

Trust in the LORD with all your heart,
And lean not on your own understanding;
In all your ways acknowledge Him,
And He shall direct your paths.

Proverbs 3:5–6, NKJV

When I tried to understand all this,
  it was oppressive to me
till I entered the sanctuary of God;
  then I understood their final destiny.

Psalm 73:16–17

When the challenges, hardships and tragedies of life come—and they will come—where do we turn? To our own logic? To what we think is best? Or will we turn to Him? Only in the refuge of His presence can we find true peace, healing and strength for this life. Jesus knows and cares. Will we trust Him? Perhaps one of His greatest love lessons (and hardest) is to live out Psalm 56:11: "In *God I trust*" (emphasis added).

Oh, to love Him with abandoned dependence! In times of crisis, do we trust God alone for deliverance? Our Mozambican family can teach us so much about this. Most Westerners always have a "Plan B." We have so many sources to which we can turn for deliverance: money, health insurance, good medical care/hospitals/medicine, retirement plans, credit cards, etc. . . . These things are not evil or necessarily wrong—God can and does use these things for His glory—but when we trust money or medicine more than trusting God, we allow these things to be our savior. Something powerful happens when we refuse to trust in alternatives for relief; when we look to Jesus and say, "No! My trust is not in money or medicine! You alone, O God, are my deliverer!"

In Mozambique, the average person has no access to medicine or quality health care. If someone gets sick, the believers fervently fast and pray, knowing Jesus is the only source of hope and deliverance. And guess what? Many people get healed. Not all instantly, and some people do not get healed at all. But when believers continually turn to Jesus with expectant, dependent hearts, the Kingdom of heaven comes to earth!

> My soul, wait silently for God alone,
> For my expectation is from Him.
> He only is my rock and my salvation;
> He is my defense;
> I shall not be moved.
> In God is my salvation and my glory;
> The rock of my strength,
> And my refuge, is in God.
> Trust in Him at all times, you people;
> Pour out your heart before Him;
> God is a refuge for us.
> Selah.
>
> Psalm 62:5–8, NKJV

A testimony...

Manuel

We have a new boy named Manuel (four years old, but he looks and acts like he is two). He is having a good adjustment with all things considered. His mother died a few weeks ago, and his father abandoned the boys to a distant cousin. After a week of abuse and neglect, a local Iris pastor told the family about our center. Manuel and his brother were ours the next day. At first Manuel had the typical blank stare—we call it the "orphan spirit." But after a few days, he was smiling and playing. Jesus has provided a huge, loving family for him. I love watching the transformation. Manuel is realizing that he will always have plenty to eat. He has fresh, clean water to drink, new clothes that will not be taken from him, new friends teaching him Jesus songs while they play and some strange white lady always wanting to hug, kiss and cuddle him!

Prayer requests

Revival

Pray for our Pemba church—we are very excited about the heavenly visions and salvations we see happening, but we know there is more! Please pray for a greater hunger and desperation for Jesus. Please also pray for the evangelism teams. Every week we have teams going forth from our center to preach the Gospel to unreached Makua villages. This month we sent one team to tour northern Mozambique, preaching and encouraging the local churches. We have heard amazing testimonies of what God is doing in the bush.

Safety

Violence is increasing around our base. Last month one of our missionaries was slashed with a knife (cutting her bag strap and her arm) when she and another missionary were walking between our centers. A few days later, another girl from a local hotel was attacked. Last week someone tried to steal a guitar and camera from a young YWAMer [Youth With A Mission] who was walking with a huge group (which has always been safe before). We got the guitar back, but some people in the villages began beating the thief mercilessly. The YWAM team thought the villagers were going to kill him. It was a very ugly scene. We took the thief to the police for his own protection, but the police sometimes beat people, too. It is just another hideous reminder of sin's havoc in Africa.

Malaria

After fifteen months of great health, I experienced the misery of malaria. I was not alone. In the past month more than a fifth of our missionaries, a sixth of our kids and a tenth of our pastors have been sick with malaria. One missionary [Ashlee] was dangerously close to being evacuated to South Africa, so we held a prayer vigil over her all night. We took turns praying in the Spirit over her for a few hours. By the next morning Ashlee was able to sit up in bed and eat (the first time in three days). Glory! Please pray for a malaria-free zone over the Christians of Pemba.

Every day in Mozambique is a gift from God. God's heart and revival cannot be stopped, nor should they be slowed down or denied! Onward and upward we go.

His and therefore yours,
Teisa and Pemba family

Life principles: Deeper still

When Ezekiel was drawn by the angel of the Lord, deeper and deeper into the river of God, eventually the water came up to his waist, and it was a river he could not cross. The water was deep enough to swim in. Ezekiel had come to the place of *immersion*. This is the place I am continually contending to be in my life. I pray there would be a holy hunger that rises up in you, too, so that you would begin contending for a life of full submersion and enter the place where your will is totally subject to His will, your spirit subject to His Spirit. This is the place where the miracles can begin to happen.

The more immersed in God you become, the less of a grip "normal" life has on you. Circumstances throw themselves against you, but you remain unmoved. When you are deep in God's river, even the tragedies of life that inevitably come only force you deeper into Him.

We had a horrible tragedy in Mozambique several years ago that became the turning point of our ministry. Everything fell apart around us. Rolland contracted cerebral malaria, and I discovered I had multiple sclerosis. Plus, my daughter contracted malaria. And at the same time, the Marxists repossessed all our ministry buildings, and we were thrown out onto the street—our family of four, plus all the kids we were caring for.

I was tired and I was angry! I heard the voice of the angel of the Lord beckoning me to come deeper into God's presence, but at the same time, I was hurting badly—life was practically unbearable. We had no way to control the circumstances we found ourselves in, and at that time, we were caring for 320 homeless children we had picked up from street corners, under bridges and from the garbage dump. They all called us Mama and Papa and had become utterly dependent on us.

We retreated to the last building we had—our tiny office twenty miles away from our former base. We had one toilet between all of us, nowhere to sleep and no food. I was angry with God! I prayed and said, "God, You're mean! How could You let this happen?" I could not understand why He would let the Marxists take our building and leave us homeless. I didn't get it.

But when all hell breaks loose, you have a choice. You can either go deeper into the river of God's presence or you can retreat from the water and try to figure out what to do in your own strength. For a long while I was in the twilight zone between these two places, yet the Spirit of God was continually calling me deeper.

I can't say that I was full of faith at that time—I wasn't. I desperately needed a miracle. Later that day, God in His mercy provided one by supernaturally multiplying the food brought to us by a friend.[4] That day I went a little deeper in Him. In fact, I took a plunge, because I had seen God do a great miracle right in front of our eyes.

The deeper you get into the river of God's glory, the more you discover how *good* He really is. He turns out to be so much more beautiful than you can imagine. Don't worry today if you feel you are in over your head. Something fresh and powerful can begin to flow through your life when you allow yourself to soak in the river of God. Surrender to Him and let the river flow! Go deeper still.

[4] See story in the "About Iris Ministries" section at the end of the book.

One Sunday in Pemba photos

1. A man raised from the dead and delivered from demons and alcohol

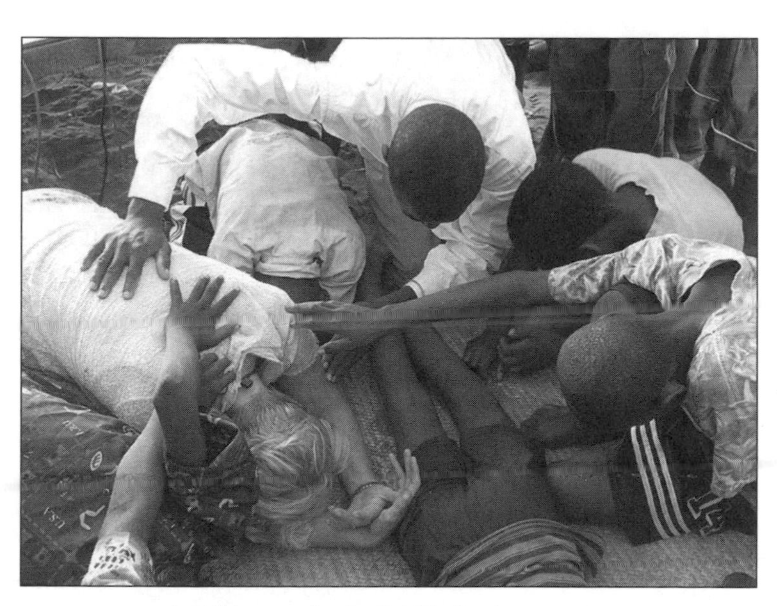

2. Children praying for Heidi before her message

3. Our hundreds of children in Pemba, gathered to hear the Word

4. Baptizing more ex-Moslems in the Indian Ocean

Update from Rolland and Heidi photo

Heidi with Crispen, who was given a heavenly visitation

Chapter 11

What Does Love Look Like?

June 2006

Update from Rolland

Posted June 2, 2006 @ 4:01 P.M.

The victory

It's absolutely amazing to be receiving so much support from all over the world as a result of your spreading our news through your networks and connections! Clearly, Jesus has some creative options and is using them in response to the prayers of so many.

We were trying to meet with the Frelimo political party chief in Pemba for days, but we were refused and ignored, even when Heidi and our staff waited in his office for hours. Finally, one afternoon his secretary was gone, and Heidi and our provincial pastor just marched up to the chief's office and persuaded him to listen. On the way she met the author of the derogatory article, who was very ill at ease and embarrassed.

The party chief did not respond well at first and in fact kept threatening us, saying that not only would the party not retract their story but that they were going to print even more against us in the newspaper. After quite a long time, though, there was a sudden, big shift. Heidi had been explaining our hearts and work, softly and in tears. We are for the country, have nothing against the party and simply want to love and help. She explained what we do with children and education, and Pastor José boldly told of our evangelism all over the province. We have no political agenda and want to do good to everyone we meet, in the name of Jesus. As they kept sharing our motivation and purposes in Mozambique, the chief softened and broke. He believes us, he said, and confessed to having a hard knot in his heart over all this. He said he was so relieved to be free of this hardness and that this had become a great day in his life.

It seems that some pastors or people in our Iris churches somewhere had been stirring up some political activism under our name without our knowledge or involvement, and word had gotten back to the capital. The president of the country himself became concerned and had ordered the country's justice department to investigate Iris. He also was the one who asked the newspaper in Pemba to publish this article! A lot of people got inflamed, using the incident as a means to resist our presence in Mozambique.

But this chief of the Frelimo Party (the party we were accused of undermining) in Pemba melted before Heidi and now has promised to have another article published, correcting the previous article. We haven't seen that article yet, however, and are waiting for the result. The situation right up until almost five o'clock on Tuesday was actually very critical and looking very dangerous for Iris, more than we had communicated. The chief's reversal was huge.

But Jesus had something else up His powerful, creative sleeve. Yesterday Heidi arrived at the Pemba airport to fly out on another speaking trip and very uncharacteristically was early. She was there at the airport just as the president's wife and entourage landed for a big Frelimo political event in Pemba. As the provincial governor and others who had been attacking us looked on, Heidi connected with local leaders who were putting on a dance at the airport to welcome the VIPs. Heidi was enthusiastically asked to dance with the children in their Frelimo T-shirts and soon was blending in completely with their program, all of which was broadcast on national television. She got on famously with everyone and clearly showed that she and Iris had no problems with the party and the people of Pemba. All this, of course, will get back to the president.

Our Moslem friends in Pemba have been seen meeting with the instigators of the anti-Iris reports, but they are dealing with huge pressure from their families and the Moslem community.

We do need very much to address these issues among our pastors and church people. As in China, believers need to build a reputation for being the best citizens, the most reliable, honest, hard-working people around who will be good for the country. We have only one life to give, and in such situations we need to give it for the Gospel and not for secondary issues. . . . We are sure that the vast majority of our church people have no desire to use Iris for political purposes.

So Jesus is doing what only He can do, as usual, and we trust Him to be with us always in everything. We love all of you for the way you have lifted us up before the King and have encouraged us so overwhelmingly. We will keep sending you updates.

Much, much love in Him!
Rolland and Heidi

News briefs from Iris bases
Lichinga, Mozambique
Posted June 27, 2006 @ 5:42 P.M., filed under Iris Bases, Mozambique, Lichinga

We want to thank Jesus for showing us how to be the fragrance of His heart in so many ways. On Saturday, two Yao sisters (also young mothers), accepted Jesus into their hearts after Annelisa and I (Antoinette) had shared the Gospel with them in their dirt courtyard, shelling peas together. We had never been to their home before and it was heartwarming to have all four or five sisters sitting around us in a circle, listening. Only two of them came to the decision of accepting Jesus as their Lord and Savior, but what a party there has been in heaven over Helena and Lucia! Helena is an orphan, so in that sense she must have been integrated into this family. She now has her own child and was so touched when she heard that Annelisa and I are starting a children's village here in Lichinga. May she and her sister follow Jesus with their whole hearts.

Praise the Lord

- That we are now in the process of purchasing land for the children's village!
- That the elderly, Portuguese owner seems to be a very generous, honest person. A joy to deal with!
- That we now have a house, belonging to the same owner, in which we shall be staying rent-free while we build on the property—which is just across the road.

Prayer requests

- That the paperwork for the land be dealt with quickly, not taking three months as usual.
- That our family would have wisdom as we disciple new believers.
- That the new believers would be filled with a hunger to be holy like Jesus is holy and to grow in Him.

Right now we just have the Wilcox family serving the Lord as long-term missionaries here in Lichinga (a happy team of eight!). But how joyful we are that we can live for Him in this way, knowing full well that our co-workers shall be sent in God's perfect timing. Please really pray that especially Mozambicans would be raised up to help in the harvest field and the children's village. We love you all heaps and thank you for your prayers and support. They mean a lot to us and to Jesus!

May He draw you ever closer into His loving heart,
The Wilcox Family

Matola, Mozambique
Posted June 27, 2006 @ 5:16 P.M., filed under Iris Bases, Mozambique, Matola

November last year we started to rent a house in Matola (close to Maputo), not knowing what God had in mind for us, except the desire in our hearts to work with HIV-positive children. Since that time, God has blessed us enormously. Now, only half a year later, we have a ministry here with seven children with ages ranging from seven months to eleven years. The eighth child will come next week. Two other children have gone to heaven already, but not before they at least experienced what it is to be loved and cared for.

Benedito, eleven years old, came to live with us in April. First he was so sick and upset that he had to stay in the hospital. He had a "witchcraft cord" around his foot and was not very interested in Jesus. But he has changed! He is such a happy boy and sits in church next to the pastor. He is fully alive.

With eight children our house will be full, but God has told us not to limit His work—not to put human walls around it (see Zechariah 2:1–5)—and has opened the doors already to buy a bigger house so that in the future we can house 25 children.

We work with a team of mostly Mozambican pastors and educators who have a heart for God and for the children. Denika (from the States) works with us also in the area of church planting and evangelism.

Please pray for us, the children and the new house. We need to renovate the house so that we can move in soon—and so that more children can come.

Corrie, Denika and Mozambican staff and children

India

Posted June 27, 2006 @ 5:57 P.M., filed under Iris Bases, Iris India

[For safety purposes we cannot share actual names or places of the work of this base.]

This is a pastor's wife's story (we will call her Sheila). Sheila was diagnosed with TB and was dying, as doctors had done all they could do. She and her husband were in such medical debt that all the other pastors from churches we have planted came alongside and poured out money to them (even though it was not much). The love and prayer covering was stunning. God showed up and touched Sheila so much so that she is up and about! She has strength and hope flooding through her because of the support of not just her family but the Body of Christ at large. Is not the Lord's way so marvelous? Our God is practical as well as miraculous! Let's love His ways!

Prayer request

That we may hear Him well in everything, and in all our ways acknowledge Him.

Zimpeto, Mozambique

Posted June 27, 2006 @ 5:45 P.M., filed under Iris Bases, Mozambique, Zimpeto

The highlight of our center the past month was the wedding of Betinho Puze and Liz Lazar. This was the first full orphan of the ministry to marry a daughter of a missionary (now a missionary in her own right).

The ceremony was conducted during church. Yollanda from Petra ministries blessed the wedding, then guests were seated at tables in the front of the church, and 350 children joined us all for a chicken-and-chips lunch.

Liz and Betinho were blessed greatly by being able to share lunch with their very big family! They now live and minister on the Zimpeto base. Steve and Ros are blessed to now have another son! This is truly how God lifts the poor out of the dust and seats them with princes (princesses) in heavenly places. What an awesome God we serve!

We love to pray and see God provide for our kids here at Zimpeto. This last month, due to the cold, we needed more blankets but did not have the cash to purchase them. The next day, after we prayed, a visitor donated enough cash for us to walk into the store and purchase enough blankets to keep our 350 kids warm during these cold months.

God's presence is evident during the regular weekly outreaches to the villages surrounding Zimpeto. Local folk never tire of hearing about salvation. The Holy Spirit is constantly at work, touching lives, convicting hearts and bringing souls into the Kingdom. Churches are being planted and flourishing. The harvest is more than ready! Hallelujah!

Agree with us in prayer:

- We are waiting on God for His strategy for our older youth. As their "parents," we are looking at different ways God might open to be able to provide for the future of these awesome youth.
- Having established some effective structures in the center, we are now ready to receive more sick and dependent children and babies. Agree with us in prayer that God will give us the hidden treasures of darkness to pour out His love over these abandoned, malnourished and unwanted treasures.

We want to be found coloring outside the lines, pushing the boundaries of tradition and living lives that are radically obedient and totally available to our awesome God!

Dondo, Mozambique

Posted June 27, 2006 @ 5:58 P.M., filed under Iris Bases, Mozambique, Dondo

God is restoring the spiritual atmosphere in Dondo, and we are seeing great transformation in this place. Our children once lived in clay houses. Today they have a house that gives them security. They have educators and missionaries that love and care for them. We now hear their voices filled with joy!

Right now we are building classrooms for our Bible school and dormitories for our students and pastors, as well as a house where we can care for girls. God is truly blessing us. Being confident in His love and care, we are praying that He sends us missionaries to help in the area of our medical clinic, as well as someone to help with electronics (preferably people who speak Portuguese—especially for the clinic). We are praying also for the construction of our fence and the church and to buy a large truck and car for our base.

God's supernatural power is manifest among us. Our evangelism team was praying with some people, and a woman asked that we pray for her to have a son. She had been married for eight years but was not able to have children. In the Mozambican culture, a couple need to have children to be honored (especially the men). We prayed for her, and God gave her a son. Glory to God!

What does love look like?

[Teisa Miller, Iris missionary]

The days, weeks and months fly by in a blessed whirlwind at our Pemba center. Many of you have been praying for the political situation that caused considerable tension for our staff in Pemba. We believe things are shifting for His glory, but please continue to pray with us for a breakthrough with the local Moslem authorities and newspapers. I am not going to share too much about this; instead, I want to share a little story and another love lesson from Jesus. . . .

I love having my daily time with Jesus on the beach (our Pemba beach is incredibly beautiful). As I walk, He and I often play this fun little game. God highlights certain shells scattered in the sand, and I get to guess what each shell represents. As the Holy Spirit leads, I hold the shell in my hand and pray for a certain person or situation. When done, I usually toss the shell back in the ocean (returning the burden to God), or I keep it to give to someone and maybe pray with them, encourage them, etc.

One morning, about a month ago, I was out taking my walk with Jesus, and I was ready to play our game. A few shells caught my eye, but I felt this impression not to touch them. I thought, *Hmm, this is weird. Why can't I touch them?* No answer, so I tried again. The same feeling of conviction came over me as I reached down. *Okay, no shells today, Lord.* I sat myself in the sand, determined to pray, but no strong direction came. *Okay, I will simply worship,* I thought. But I could not even worship. I thought this was all very strange, but I figured I just needed to simply wait and listen. After some time, I squeezed my feet deeper in the sand, and my hands began to fidget. As I scooped up a handful of sand and let it escape through my fingers, the Lord spoke to my heart: *So are My expressions of love for My Bride.*

Wow! Suddenly, the sand around me became extremely important. Every grain had meaning! In my hand alone there were thousands; under my feet were billions; each tiny grain represented a facet of His love! How limitless is the love of Abba! How great, how unfathomable, how precious are His thoughts of love for us. Thoroughly undone by the revelation, I began rolling around in the sand. Eventually, I landed on my belly, facedown, and I began examining these treasures of love more closely. Guess what? Each grain is different from the next. . . .

This has had me thinking for weeks. If each expression of His love is so unique, what about ours? What does our love look like? Shouldn't our love for Him reflect His creativity and awesomeness? Or do we do the same things day after day, saying the same things, singing the same songs? God forbid! Without careful devotion, our love for Him can so easily become stagnant, status-quo—dare I say, boring!

> "As the Father has loved me, so have I loved you. Now remain in my love."
>
> John 15:9

> Jesus replied, " 'Love the Lord your God with all your heart and with all your soul and with all your mind.' This is the first and greatest commandment. And the second is like it: 'Love your neighbor as yourself.' "
>
> Matthew 22:37–39

What about our expressions of love for our neighbor? What do we see in the eyes of the person standing before us? How can we reach him or her with the love of God? By asking these questions, Jesus invites us on an incredible journey of discovery. He desires to open our eyes to see His love with new vision.

For Julianna, love looks like a home

I met Julianna way back when I was just visiting Iris during my 2004 "job interview." Her situation broke my heart. At 33 years old, Julianna was the mother of six and grandmother of two. Her "husband" abandoned her, making her the sole provider for her family. Upon retuning to Pemba in 2005, I started supporting Julianna.

About eight months ago, Julianna moved out of her sister's home to escape an abusive man. With a humble offering from missionaries in Pemba, Julianna moved into a new home. She was so grateful for the offering, and she never told us anything more about her house. We assumed it was a typical Mozambican mud/cement house. But we were wrong.

In May, Yonnie (my housemate) and I went to visit Julianna. We were shocked by what we saw. Her house was only a third done: The roof was incomplete, the house had no doors and the walls were full of large holes, leaving Julianna and her family exposed daily to the elements.

It became obvious what love looked like for this family. For the past two months, we have carried sand, rocks and other building material to her house. Currently we are cementing the outer walls. Progress is slow but steady. We are still believing God for $600 to complete her house (donations can be made for Julianna's house via MIA—www.mia.org). We are so excited about Jesus' lavish expression of love for Julianna. After we finish her home, we have many other women at risk in our Pemba church who also need new roofs, repairs or new homes. He always has more than enough!

> Religion that God our Father accepts as pure and faultless is this: to look after orphans and widows in their distress and to keep oneself from being polluted by the world.
>
> James 1:27

For Lourdis, love looks like a **family**

A few weeks ago, we welcomed another new baby girl to our Pemba center. Just like Maria, Lourdis Luis was brought to us by her grandmother. Her story is tragically similar. Lourdis's mother died two days after giving birth. Her grandmother did not know the father; therefore, she began caring for the baby. Her grandmother also shared how Lourdis was the fifteenth baby born to her daughter and how twelve of her siblings had died. Born weighing 3.5 pounds, Lourdis lived on watered-down cornmeal mixture with some sugar and water. Upon arrival at our center, at six weeks old, Lourdis still weighed 3.5 pounds. She was so shockingly malnourished, many of us thought, *Dear Jesus, we just lost Maria, now we have this tiny, sick baby who might also die.* We began to declare, "Lourdis will live and not die," every time we held and prayed for her.

Today, Lourdis weighs eight pounds, and she grows stronger day by day. She even has a tiny double chin now! She is a feisty girl who loves to be held. If you try to put her down, she will make her displeasure known! Lourdis is our dearest crybaby. She is dearly loved and enjoys being the most sought-after addition to our family.

> "I will not leave you as orphans; I will come to you."
>
> John 14:18

> A father to the fatherless, a defender of widows,
> is God in his holy dwelling.
> God sets the lonely in families.
>
> Psalm 68:5–6

***For the Warriors, love looks like a* restaurant**

This is a very flawed metaphor, but the Warriors understand it ("the Warriors" are my boys' dorm—eight of the mightiest little men in Africa). Almost every day my boys look up at me with their adorable faces and say, "Mama Teisa, *Restaurante hoje*?" ("Can we go to the restaurant today?") Going to the restaurant means several things for them: It means freedom and playtime away from the center where they play 24-7 if someone does not take them out. It means Coca-Cola and yummy food like ice cream or chicken, which is a huge treat for children who survived starvation and extreme poverty. It means education, because we often have an object lesson before the food treat; therefore, the Warriors are learning to love to learn! Most of all, I believe the Warriors love going out to a restaurant (or my house, Heidi's house, etc.) because it means quality time with someone who loves them.

> "And whoever welcomes a little child like this in my name welcomes me."
>
> Matthew 18:5

> "And if anyone gives even a cup of cold water to one of these little ones because he is my disciple, I tell you the truth, he will certainly not lose his reward."
>
> Matthew 10:42

***For the guys at the missions school and our Mozambican pastors, love looks like* holding hands**

In Africa, people hold hands with people of the same sex, not the opposite sex. Men holding hands with men is an accepted expression of friendship. In Western culture, most men find the very idea of holding another man's hand unacceptable and repulsive. But in Africa, if a man is walking in the same direction with a friend, he would offer his hand and the two would stroll along together. To refuse a brother's hand is a great insult. Yet, conversely, imagine how challenging this might be for a Western man. Knowing this, it brings me great joy to see our Western brothers strolling along with African brothers, sharing their clothes, sharing their food, sharing their lives, hand in hand. What a picture of love.

> This is how we know what love is: Jesus Christ laid down his life for us. And we ought to lay down our lives for our brothers. If anyone has material possessions and sees his brother in need but has no pity on him, how can the love of God be in him? Dear children, let us not love with words or tongue but with actions and in truth.
>
> 1 John 3:16–18

> "The King will reply, 'I tell you the truth, whatever you did for one of the least of these brothers of mine, you did for me.' "
>
> Matthew 25:40

***For Jesus, love looked like a* cross**

The cross was the ultimate "I LOVE YOU!" It was the Father saying to the world, "This is how much I love you"; the Son saying to the Father, "This is how much I love You"; the Bridegroom saying to His Bride, "This is how much I love you."

For every true believer in Jesus Christ, love will always look like a cross. The cross is our home. We know that we are crucified with Christ (see Galatians 2:20), but we have an uncanny way of crawling off the cross and seeking comfort elsewhere. But the fullness of life can be found nowhere else. Only in the declaration, "I want to know Christ and the power of his resurrection and the fellowship of sharing in his sufferings" (Philippians 3:10), can we be like Him.

> I take, O cross, thy shadow
> For my abiding place
> I ask no other sunshine than
> The sunshine of His face
> Content to let the world go by
> To know no gain or loss
> My sinful self my only shame
> My glory in the cross.
>
> Elizabeth C. Clephane (public domain)

Every morning that I wake up, I thank God for the opportunity to love the Lord and love people in Pemba, Mozambique. As the journey continues, I realize that time is so short. There is so much more that the Lord desires to do here in demonstrating His infinite love. His heart is yearning to be made known to every person, until all men come to the knowledge of His saving grace. Just like Jesus said, this truly is our bread—to finish His work, making His name known to the people whom He loved so deeply and for whom He gave His life.

Muito Amor,
Teisa

Life principles: Are you blind?

I went through a period of time where I longed to see God heal the blind. In fact, I was so excited about what God might do that wherever I went I would look out for blind people, just so I could pray for them. If I was driving my truck down the street and I spotted a blind person, I would slam on the brakes, leap out, grab the blind person and pray for him or her, there and then. It was okay because the person never saw me coming!

In Africa there are many more people who are blind than in the West. They are everywhere you go, so I had a lot of practice praying for them. Then, one day, I was in a mud-hut church. It was a swelteringly hot day. We were worshiping God together when I noticed another blind person being led into the meeting. I was quite excited, thinking, *Here is another opportunity. Maybe God will heal this lady.* When I took hold of her and began to pray, a sudden wave of supernatural compassion engulfed me, and I began sobbing over her. I sobbed my heart out until God touched this lady, and *bang*—she fell backward onto the mud floor.

Looking down at her, lying in the dirt, I could see her totally white, unseeing eyes. But, as I continued to stare, I saw her eyes turn from white to gray to beautiful brown, and she blinked as God restored her sight. I was so excited. As she realized she could see, she began screaming in excitement, too. She didn't get up off the floor; she just lay there shouting in amazement. I managed to ask her, "What's your name?" and to my surprise she answered, "Mama Ida [Heidi]." "Oh," I said. "That's my name, too!"

A couple of days later I was in the next village in another hot mud hut. This time I had with me my good friend Dr. Guy Chevreau. Guy has a doctorate in theology and was following me around, researching for his book *Turnings* and making notes on the revival in Mozambique. While he was sitting, writing copiously, another blind lady came to me for prayer. I began hugging this lady, and again compassion overcame me. I wept over this lady for a long time until suddenly she began exclaiming loudly, "Oh, you are wearing a black shirt." "Yes, that's right," I said. "I can see, I can see!" she shouted. I turned around and called to Guy, "Stop writing! This lady can see!" He had missed the whole thing! It made me laugh to think that he was sitting writing about revival while God was busy giving a blind lady her sight!

I took this lady outside to test her eyesight and told her to go and fetch a bucket I could see some distance away. She went right to it and brought it to me. Then I asked her, "What's your name?" She replied, "Mama Ida!" I thought to myself, *Oh wow! Two blind Mama Idas in a couple of days. That's amazing!*

A day later I had moved on to the next village. I was so excited by this time that I was saying, "Where are the blind? Bring me the blind." In response, a very old lady was led toward me by a guy in rags. They were beggars, of course—that's how blind people are forced to live in Mozambique. I prayed for her, and she fell backward into the dirt. Right away she began screaming, "I can see! I can see!" The church congregation was ecstatic because they all knew her, so they began shouting, "Mama Ida can see!"

I couldn't believe my ears at first. I got down in the dirt next to this lady and whispered, "What is your name?" She said, "They just told you my name. It's Mama Ida! What's yours?" "It's Mama Ida," I replied with glazed eyes.

This was just too much of a coincidence. *O God,* I prayed, *what does this mean?* Do you know what He said to me? *You're blind!* I was shocked. I began to argue with God: *God, that's not nice! I feed the poor, thousands of them.* (I can't believe I told God this.) *I work in the slums; I feed widows and orphans!* I was trying to explain to God that I was not blind.

What is wrong with us? If God tells us something, then it's definitely true! Finally, I stopped arguing with God and surrendered. "If I am blind, God, then I want to see." He said to me, *I am giving you eye salve, and I'm causing your eyes to be opened. And I am going to give you eye salve for the Church. My Church's eyes have been blurred. They have been slow to see. But I am opening the eyes of the Church.*

Before that day I did very little traveling to speak at churches outside of Africa. I went occasionally, but it was always with great reluctance. I loved my nation, Mozambique, but if I am honest, I did not love the Western Church, because I did not think the people were hungry. The Lord used these strange healings to show me how blind I was and how much the Western Church also needs to see—to see what God is doing among the poorest people on earth, to see the poor around them. God is passionate for the poor of every nation—the poor of the West, who often go in disguise, as well as the poor of Africa.

That day I moved a little deeper into the heart of God; I gained a little more understanding. Something in me that had resisted what God wanted to do was broken. Are you blind? Will you allow God to apply His eye salve to your eyes so that you can see what He sees?

Chapter 12

The Long-Awaited Harvest

July 2006

Heidi's boilerplate

Posted July 1, 2006 @ 3:48 P.M.

Thank you for keeping in touch. Thank you for praying for us. We have just had an amazing conference in Nampula. Two deaf-mutes were healed! The whole village knew them, so these beautiful miracles caused quite a stir among the people. My favorite meeting was outdoors one night when the presence of God came upon us and the people fell to their knees before Jesus. Hundreds of Moslems gave their hearts to God. We also had a joyful group wedding with fourteen couples joining their lives in holy matrimony. After the weddings, there was exuberant song and dance celebrating King Jesus as hundreds of new believers were baptized.

However, I have a hunger for Jesus that is satisfied only as I find more children. In the past few days we have been enriched with three new treasures—children given to us to love and care for. As I watch Emelyn hold Lourdis, our new tiny baby, I feel God's intense pleasure. Lourdis was starving to death after her mother died, but we got her in time. She is a gift to us from Jesus. Helena, one of our twelve-year-old girls at our Zimpeto base, just died of cerebral malaria. Daily we understand both joy and suffering. Life is full of emotions. Mother Teresa has helped me through her writings to make sense of much I had trouble articulating: "Hungry for love, He looks at you. Thirsty for kindness, He begs from you. Naked for loyalty, He hopes in you. Sick and imprisoned for friendship, He wants from you. Homeless for shelter in your heart, He asks of you. Will you be that one to Him?"[5] We can find the face of God in the poor (see Matthew 25:45). We do what we do for Him, in Jesus, through Jesus, with Jesus, to Jesus. We make ourselves totally available to Him. May you know the glory of His love today. Please stop for the one.

Much love in Jesus,
Heidi

The long-awaited harvest

[Erik Shipley, one of Iris's long-term staff at Pemba]
Posted July 1, 2006 @ 3:46 P.M.

> Do not be deceived, God is not mocked; for whatever a man sows, that he will also reap. For he who sows to his flesh will of the flesh reap corruption, but he who sows to the Spirit will of the Spirit reap everlasting life. And let us not grow weary while doing good, for in due season we shall reap if we do not lose heart. Therefore, as we have opportunity, let us do good to all, especially to those who are of the household of faith.
>
> Galatians 6:7–10, NKJV

It's a typical Tuesday afternoon at Iris Ministries in Pemba. As the sun burns brightly on yet another hot and humid African day, Heidi is hidden under the shade of our massive striped green-and-white tent, preparing to pour out her heart to her ever-increasing

[5] Mother Teresa, *In the Heart of the World: Thoughts, Prayer and Stories* (Novato, Calif.: New World Library, 1997).

family. Stretched out across the tent is a sea of hundreds of faces—black, white, Asian and brown, from twelve nations of the earth, all gathered to hear the Word of the Lord. The second Iris Ministries Holy Given missions school is taking place, and it's a beautiful sight to see so many Westerners interspersed among the local Mozambican pastors and children. Truly God is raising up the once-broken nation of Mozambique to be a light to the whole world and the training ground for a mighty army of laid-down lovers that shall fill the earth with His glory.

Yet, on this particular day, Heidi is understandably tired. Iris Ministries has been under the most severe attack that it has ever endured, and just before the service, Heidi was given some more bad news. Not only was she facing death threats against herself and other Mozambican staff, but some local people were also pressing a lawsuit over issues with wages that the previous contractor had embezzled. On top of all of this, she just found out that the daughter of one of our Iris Ministries pastors had died. On this day, all seemed to go wrong and there was no hope on the horizon—that is, until God stepped in!

As Heidi began to preach on her favorite subject—love—she was noticeably exhausted from all of the recent stress and in need of relief. When all seemed to be hopeless, away in the distance came the sound of singing. It was not the sound of mourning or sadness, but the sound of great joy. As soon as Heidi turned her head, in marched triumphantly the widows from my local gardening program with their very first harvest! Each of them was carrying a head of lettuce or spinach or onions or beets. Each of them was smiling from ear to ear and dancing and singing to the Lord with all of her might.

Although in the West it would be considered rude to interrupt a church service in progress, Heidi is well acquainted with the event-oriented culture of Mozambique and freely welcomed the women to testify to the school about what God had done in their lives. They all spoke of the same thing. They came to Iris Ministries many months ago, lost, broken, sick and poor, with no hope. Many of them were Moslems and came only because they heard that there was a program they could join in order to get food for their suffering families. Yet all of them testified to the joy of meeting Jesus Christ and being transformed by His infinite love and mercy. All of them were thankful to have a Savior who took away their sins and gave them a living hope amid their hardships, which are beyond what any of us in the West can ever comprehend.

In many ways, their hearts were like the fields in which they have been working for the last five months. When they came to Iris Ministries, their hearts were hard and full of rocks and weeds. Many of them had weeds so deep that they seemed impossible to pull out. But day by day, with the patient and careful work of the Master Vinedresser, God the Father has been working on their hearts to pull out the weeds, throw away the rocks and prepare the same soil that once was richly cultivated by the devil for evil purposes, to plant His precious seed of the eternal Word of God. Then, over time, He has watered the soil with His Spirit and shone the sunlight of His glory each day until the seed has finally sprouted up from the earth into a harvest of righteousness.

> And He said, "The kingdom of God is as if a man should scatter *seed on the ground*, and should sleep by night and rise by day, and the seed should sprout and grow, he himself does not know how. *For the earth yields crops by itself*: first the blade, then the head, after that the full grain in the head. But when the grain ripens, immediately he puts in the sickle, *because the harvest has come*."
>
> Mark 4:26–29, NKJV, emphasis added

This is truly the Kingdom of almighty God! Every day we scatter seeds into the earth, searching desperately for good soil that is prepared to receive it with joy and bear fruit. Every day the Lord sends us people whose hearts are ready-ground to hear the Word of God and be saved. Sometimes the harvest takes many months to come to fruition, but with patient endurance, God sends the rains from heaven, and sure enough, the harvest does come, right on time!

Such has been the case with many of our construction workers here at Iris Ministries. Like the widows, they are Moslems, and they began with hearts that were not ready to hear the Word of God. Many of them were raised to hate Christians, and if one of their family members converts, he or she is often excommunicated or even stoned. Yet, day after day, we fearlessly preach the Gospel to these workers, letting the precious love of God work through the Holy Spirit to soften their hardened hearts until the Word of God can finally find an entrance point in their lives. Sometimes it takes many months, but the important thing is that the presence of God is in our midst, and we are confident that God is able to work through His Spirit to call the elect into His Kingdom.

With this confidence, we always wait eagerly to see the harvest come forth. Sure enough, this spiritual harvest came forth in the very same week as the natural harvest among the widows! In one service, thirty to forty workers came forward for the altar call to give their lives to Jesus Christ, wholly giving their lives to the King of righteousness. These people know the potential consequences of a public confession of faith in Christ, yet they know the great supernatural joy that God has planted in their hearts—which they cannot explain and which was never made available to them by the god of the Moslems whom they used to serve. The harvest has truly come, and it is a precious thing to eat of its fruits!

Nampula meetings with Global Awakening

Later on that very same week, a team from Randy Clark's ministry, Global Awakening, embarked on a four-day outreach to Nampula, a city six hours southwest of Pemba by truck. Nampula is also a highly concentrated Moslem area and still in much need of the light of the Gospel. Two nights before they left, the team members asked me if I would go along with them to help them translate and also to better understand the culture and people they would be ministering to. For a couple of weeks I had been praying about whether or not I was supposed to go on that trip, but I was waiting on the Lord for provision and an open door from heaven. Sure enough, the team also insisted on paying for my room and board at the hotel in which we would be staying, so at 6:00 A.M. on Wednesday, off to Nampula I went.

The Nampula conference was a typical Iris-style conference. We sent out trucks into the farthest regions of the province, bringing in the poor, the lame and the broken, inviting them to come to banquet at the Lord's table and eat. We also trucked in our pastors from all over the province to help strengthen and encourage them in the Word of God. For three days people kept coming in from the farthest of regions to hear the anointed Word being preached and to feast on the Mozambican staple diet of rice and beans. As Randy, Heidi and the team preached, hundreds of Moslems gave their lives to Christ, and many were healed of sickness and disease. Two deaf-mutes heard for the very first time when Heidi prayed for them, leading to much excitement among the local people who knew that they could not previously hear or talk. It was a great time for all as the Kingdom of God once again touched down and transformed one broken life after another.

The highlight for me was being given the privilege by Heidi to lead the children's ministry each afternoon with the Global Awakening Team. An estimated three to four hundred children came from all around the region to join us for a time of fun and games, and to hear the Word of God being preached. The team members selflessly poured themselves out to the children, leading them in relay races and games of Simon Says and Duck, Duck, Goose (or, in this culture, since they do not have any geese, Duck, Duck, Chicken!). It was probably the first time in their lives that these children had adults actually play with them and lead them in fun and games, instead of the traditional way of allowing them to run freely among themselves. The children were starving for love, and it amazed me to see how such simple games could help open up their hearts to the message we were about to preach to them.

Both afternoons, a member from the Global team preached and I interpreted in Portuguese, while a local pastor interpreted a second time in the local language of Makua. Both afternoons the simple messages were followed by an equally simple altar call, and, of course, many raised their hands to give their lives to Jesus Christ. Children know how to simply believe without doubting or analyzing. They are an example of how to receive the Gospel of the Kingdom without complicating it. I have learned here at Iris Ministries that when we preach the Gospel, we should first go to the children (especially the orphans), because they are very close to the heart of the Lord. Many times, people trying to analyze missions work think that there is no point preaching to children because they are not educated and therefore will make little impact on their nation if converted. The children of Mozambique have so often proven this theory to be wrong, often becoming our best evangelists with their childlike faith, telling their whole families and communities about Christ. Many salvations and even healings have resulted from these little ones' simple ministry.

At the end of the conference, we dedicated the new land that was recently purchased adjacent to the church for use as a new orphanage for the local Nampula orphans. The Lord has given our provincial pastor Tanueque a huge father's heart, and unbeknownst to us, he had been praying for many months for the Lord to provide an orphanage for the children he was already beginning to care for. When Heidi announced that she was about to purchase the land, he was thrilled. The Lord had answered his prayers.

Pastor Tanueque is a mighty man of God. Between himself and his wife, Florinda, they have raised seven people from the dead. He constantly travels across the country, preaching to new unreached villages each week, yet the Lord works in his heart a spirit of meekness and love for the poor that is daily demonstrated to the most broken, lost and dying people. He is an example of what a laid-down lover of God looks like and a great light to the darkest corners of the province of Nampula and all of Mozambique. Hallelujah!

Pure religion

> Pure and *undefiled* religion before God and the Father is this: to visit orphans and widows in their trouble, and to keep oneself *unspotted from the world.*
>
> James 1:27, NKJV, emphasis added

What is pure religion? What is pure Christianity? What is pure love? What is this life all about? Is it about how many people we lead to Jesus or how many churches we plant or how good a person we have been? Or is it about being so hidden in the heart of our awesome, eternal God of love that we are swallowed up in Him, so that it is no longer we who live, but Christ in us?

> "And the King will answer and say to them, 'Assuredly, I say to you, inasmuch as you did it to one of the *least of these* My brethren, *you did it to Me.*' "
>
> Matthew 25:40, NKJV, emphasis added

The reason that I am in Africa, the reason that I have come to serve Rolland and Heidi here at Iris Ministries, the reason that I am alive, is for this purpose and this purpose alone: to learn how to love like Jesus loved. Every day Jesus meets me in unexpected ways. Sometimes He is an orphan looking for love and unconditional acceptance; sometimes He is a widow desperately begging for a simple job in order to provide the basic necessities of life for her hungry children; sometimes He is another lost and broken person who just needs a hug and someone to listen. But every day I see Him in a new way.

Yes, we are seeing hundreds of Moslems come to Jesus every week; yes, we are seeing multitudes of sick people healed by the power of the Holy Spirit; yes, we are seeing the Kingdom of God come in power in the most dark and dangerous places in Mozambique. But, at the end of the day, what matters most is LOVE! I am trying to learn to be like Christ in every possible way, yet every day, I am seeing that Christ is already inside of me, and He is happy to come out and make Himself known through me to the lost and dying world around me. He is happy to use my hands to pray for the sick, my arms to love on and to hug the orphans, and my feet to go boldly anywhere to preach the Gospel of the Kingdom to whomever's heart He has prepared to hear the Good News.

> For in Christ Jesus neither circumcision nor uncircumcision avails anything, but *faith working through love.*
>
> Galatians 5:6, NKJV, emphasis added

What is "faith working through love"? Simply abiding in Christ and letting the sweetness of His presence flow through us and minister to those around us who are lost, dying and desperate for God. It is believing that what Christ accomplished for us on the cross is enough to equip us and empower us to be bright, shining lights amid a crooked and perverse generation. It is laying down our lives so that the Kingdom of God can come forth to the broken, the lost, the dying and the weak. It is changing history, one person at a time! Hallelujah!

Much love in Christ,
Erik Shipley

Hunger among the people

Heidi: posted July 28, 2006 @ 10:04 P.M.

» p. 176 » p. 176 » p. 177 » p. 177

Thousands of people ran to the bush runway, clouds of dirt flying, children laughing and singing. Rolland landed our little Cessna on the rough grass. The joy never ends! The hunger among the people brings delight to the heart of Jesus. Masses came from all over Malawi to worship the One who is altogether beautiful. Thousands have come to meet Jesus and be healed. I called all the deaf to the rickety platform to be healed. All twelve who came forward were miraculously able to hear. What a tremendous time to be alive! During each outreach, Jesus shines His love and glory on the people. We continue to plant churches in the north of Mozambique at an astounding rate. The missions students from fifteen countries have joined our Mozambican pastors and children, enabling us to do four outreaches a week. Thousands of Moslems are surrendering their hearts to Jesus.

We are believing God for more and more breakthroughs in the Holy Spirit. Love never fails. We are pressing in for more love among us.

Please keep praying for us.

Much love in Jesus,
Heidi

His grace is sufficient for us

Heidi: posted July 17, 2006 @ 8:55 P.M.

Thank you for your love and prayers. I so appreciate your keeping in touch. God has been pouring out His Holy Spirit on us in such a beautiful way. Every week I call for the deaf to come forward during the outreach, and each week any deaf person that comes forward is healed! I love watching the faces in the crowd light up with joy as they see Jesus do miracles. The village comes to the Lord, and we plant a church the following week.

In the middle of such a harvest, we have been going through

some major spiritual warfare in the last few weeks. Some of my older southern staff and I have had several death threats. Witchcraft crept in among some of the jealous leaders, so we went on a corporate fast. Our precious children fasted and prayed as well. Something broke in the spirit on Monday. There was major repentance and unity in the end. We moved into a new place in the Holy Spirit. There were visions and words from the students and pastors. God sent a purifying wave of His Holy Spirit.

Jesus reminds me that His grace is sufficient for us, for His power is made perfect in weakness (see 2 Corinthians 12:9). If we have enough of the love of Jesus, we can get through any storm. The love of Christ Jesus causes us to spend ourselves without ceasing. I will leave you with a favorite quote from Mother Teresa: "Each one of us is what he is in the eyes of God, nothing more, nothing less. We all have been created in the image of God to love and be loved."[6]

Much love in Jesus,
Heidi

Life principles: It's lunchtime!

There was once a little boy who had a packed lunch—some bread and fish—who gave it up to God and saw a great miracle (see John 6:2–13). Jesus was surrounded by a group of hungry people, and He needed to feed them. This little kid had a meager offering of food, but Jesus took it from him and God extravagantly multiplied it.

I was thinking about this. If you were God, it wouldn't be a very nice thing to do to take away a kid's lunch, would it? But here is Jesus, and He takes the boy's lunch! Kids love to eat, don't they? Most would be pretty upset if you took their lunch away.

Yet here is a multitude of people, and Jesus has a problem. There

[6] Mother Teresa, Nobel Lecture, December 11, 1979.

is a huge crowd of people who are hungry and want to be fed. I can easily visualize the scene—recently, we had a conference where there were twelve thousand people gathered in the bush. They were ravenously hungry, spiritually as well as naturally. Many people had walked three days without food to get to the meeting. They had waded through crocodile-infested water with bare feet. They slept outside on the dirt with no grass mats and no cover for four or five days because they were so desperate to get a touch from God. And God would not let them down.

No doubt Jesus looked around, spotted this little kid with his lunch and thought, *I can use him.* We are a lot like that kid. We are nothing special, naturally speaking, yet in God's eyes we are totally awesome. He can do great things with us if we will cooperate with Him. Your little lunch in the hands of God can feed a multitude!

But hear this: We have to stop looking at our lunch (because it is kind of pitiful) and look at God! Stop looking at your limited resources and start looking at the One who can multiply them. Stop looking at your life and thinking how insignificant it looks! Yield it to God, fully, totally, completely, and allow Him to multiply it.

Most people think, *That's too simple.* They have a habit of saying, "But look at me!" thinking their case is unique—that they, in some way, are uniquely disqualified from serving God and will never see Him do miraculous things through them. But when you say, "Look at me," God always responds, "But look at *Me*!"

As God worked in my life and taught me to live in His presence, eventually I stopped looking at me. Now I don't want to look at me anymore, because I *know* me! Instead, I began dwelling in the secret place of God where my heart and mind were always focused on Him and not on me. I became so overwhelmed with who God is, that I stopped worrying about me altogether.

My purpose became to keep my vision fixed on the beauty of Him, the glory of Him, the holiness of Him, the all-sufficiency of Him! In effect, I said to God, "You want my lunch? Well, here, take it! It's small and insignificant, so I don't know what You can do with it, but You're welcome!"

Guess what God did with my lunch? He planted six thousand churches in five years. He takes all the credit and the glory for this, not me. It's nothing to do with me! I just handed over what I had to the Master, and He worked a miracle.

I think if that little boy had held anything back from Jesus, he might have prevented a miracle. I'm theorizing, of course. In the same way, we cannot hold back from God. You cannot divide up your life, giving a bit to God and holding some back for yourself, just in case He doesn't show up. It's all or nothing! God doesn't do half-measures. You have to throw yourself into Him completely, holding nothing back. Then He is able to do the miraculous with your life. Then He can do what only He can do.

So please, give Him your "lunch," your life! Why do you want to hold on to it? Remember, God can do anything with anybody.

Hunger among the people photos

1. Flying over our Bible school at Bangula, Malawi

2. Cooking for our Malawi conference

3. The poor and desperate of Malawi cry out to God

4. Our Malawi national leaders worshiping at Bangula

Chapter 13

Confidence in Him

August–September 2006

From Heidi

Posted September 21, 2006 @ 7:12 P.M.

» p. 187 » p. 187 » p. 188 » p. 188

» p. 189

It is always good to hear from you. Friends are our greatest treasures in this world. I really appreciate your praying for me. I know I could not get through things in Mozambique without prayer. I love what God is doing here, but things have been super stressful financially. I believe God allows lean times so He can change whatever attitudes do not bring Him pleasure. The amazing thing is, every day somehow there is food. What a faithful God we serve.

The highlight of my month was staying in a distant mud-hut village. We dedicated two of our new churches in Nacaca and

Kampin. The village people live simple lives with nearly no outside contact. They trade their crops for whatever they need to survive. There is no medical care, running water or wells, no electricity or shops. These beautiful people had never had access to the Gospel before our teams arrived. Old tribal women wear black wooden rings under their noses as ornaments.

What a delight to see children and village elders worshiping Jesus with us in our newly dedicated mud church. Dust flew as we danced on the dirt floor, thanking God for blessing us with a place to worship Him. We visited some village houses to pray for the sick. In one house, a man was dying and could hardly walk. After we prayed for him, he beamed with joy and walked to our feast, proclaiming his healing! One man we prayed for in his hut was deaf since early childhood. He was thrilled along with all the family as Jesus opened up his ears. An old granny also laughed heartily as she was blessed with her hearing again after years of near silence.

I am off to another distant village now. Thanks for standing with us.

Love in Jesus,
Heidi

Overnight in the bush

Rolland: posted September 27, 2006 @ 10:40 A.M.

Village outreaches are Iris at its most basic. This is the core of what we do. Here is where we meet the poor, the remote, the forgotten lost sheep of the world. Here the Gospel shines deeply into the darkness, facing head-on our frail human predicament and all the despair and damage that Satan and his demons can do. Our province of Cabo Delgado, classified by missiologists as unreached and unreachable, has been a land of syncretism and witchcraft, famous for its resistance to the Gospel. But the power of the Holy

Spirit is overcoming the darkness, village by village, and tonight we are launching out again.

Our team of staff and visitors are going to pack into three trucks. After a typically intense day of meetings and business, we start pulling our gear together. We need tents, sleeping bags, mosquito spray, flashlights, drinking water and a bare minimum of personal stuff so we can stay overnight. A Mozambican team has gone on ahead with our sound equipment, a generator and a screen and projector for the *Jesus* film.

We are all loaded, but we need diesel fuel, and it takes a while to locate a station with a working compressor to fill our tires. Vehicle maintenance is a huge challenge in our very remote town of Pemba.

It's almost sundown, and we head south down our only paved highway, stopping at police checkpoints. We continue on in the dark. The air cools. The moon appears from behind clouds, casting a faint, silvery glow on the thatched mud-hut villages that come up again and again along the narrow road. Without electricity, they seem ghostly quiet and deserted until children here and there (and sometimes chickens) dart across the road in our headlights.

Then we turn off to the east, taking a dirt road that winds around trees, ditches and scrub brush and through ruts and gullies, making us appreciate again the long-travel coil suspension of our Land Rovers. This is remote. We are far from lights and telephones, shops and gas stations. We feel alone in the shadowy night, deep in the African bush. Who could be out here waiting for us?

Finally, more mud huts and a clearing appear. We slow down and carefully thread our way between huts, turning sharply back and forth and avoiding deep pits. Then suddenly, around a corner, we see the meeting. Bright images are flashing across a screen high above a crowd. Heads are silhouetted against the screen, which is showing a man commanding the attention of all those around him. The sound is crisp, carrying far through the night air. This entire village is listening to the Master also, hearing His words in their own Makua language. They have not been forgotten. The Good News has arrived.

After the film, Heidi preaches her heart out, going straight to their hearts with the Makua she has learned. Everyone responds, crowding around the platform, the flatbed of our big Mazda truck. They are jumping and dancing in clouds of blowing dust lit up by our floodlights. They are crying and shouting. And they humble themselves and pray, asking their incredibly great and merciful Savior to rescue them in every way. There is no resistance, no holding back, no indifference. They have recognized, many for the first time in their lives, what love is, and they cannot get enough.

We have been to this village before and have already begun a church here. But tonight our return visit is still a huge event. These isolated, illiterate baby believers feel connected to the outside world, and they feel so loved and encouraged that God would send all these visitors from across the world to their very own village. The meeting goes late. Our team, including some of our children from our Pemba center, are busy praying for every hungry, needy person who comes to them. The singing and testimonies continue into the night.

We pitch our tents in the dark with our flashlights, finding space in a fenced-in little courtyard of swept dirt between huts. The night is cool. The unfamiliar stars of the southern hemisphere are brilliantly arrayed in a sky far from lights and pollution. Sleep comes easily, until the drums begin. And then, until four or five in the morning, the village witch doctors persist with their chanting and drumming in a determined effort to undermine our spiritual effect on their turf.

We wake up with the chickens and brush our teeth with bottled water. The guitars come out in our group, and soft worship music floats out across the thatched roofs. The village has never had visitors like this or an occasion like this. Today we dedicate the new church, proudly built with reeds and mud, with an Iris dove and rainbow over the entrance. Everyone congregates, young and old. Children jump with excitement. Mama Ida is here to do the honors. We all press around the front door and pray with all our hearts that Jesus will fill this holy place with His presence and extend His Kingdom through all the ministry that will flow from it. With a huge grin Heidi cuts the ribbon, and everyone shouts with joy. We flood in, and soon dust is flying again as we all sing and dance with an intensity found only in Africa.

We teach, we pray, we lay hands on pastors. Some people are overcome by the power of God, shaking intensely on the ground with tears and supernatural joy. Our concentration, as always, is Jesus and Him crucified. We point everyone to the cross. We are here to impart faith, without which all our work is for nothing. Jesus alone makes all the difference. And again, there is no resistance. The witch doctors make no headway against the work of the Spirit.

We start packing up to preach in another village before returning to Pemba. But first, two children are brought to us. Their mother has died, and their father is deaf and unable to care for them. Can we bring them back to our children's center? We decide to see the father and make sure he's okay with this. So we meet with him, and of course Heidi prays for his ears. Suddenly, right there in the bright sun in front of the village leaders and everyone standing around, Jesus heals the father and he can hear! Cheers erupt. The father is grinning and overjoyed (see photo). Now everything is changed. The father can work again and take care of his children at home. And the children can stay in their village with their father, attending their very own home church. Another great day in the bush. . . .

» p. 189

We pack up, load our extra gear on our roof racks and traverse a few more miles of rough dirt road to get to another of our new village churches. Again, we impart all we can to an isolated Iris family of believers out in the bush and ask the Holy Spirit to watch over them and keep them deeply planted in the heart of Jesus. They are thrilled. By late afternoon we are back in Pemba, richer in spirit than ever. May the Lord of the harvest send many more teams into the African bush. . . .

The Word of the Lord is spreading through Cabo Delgado Province just like this, village by village, miracle by miracle. The poor and humble do not refuse so great a salvation. They do not want to live without Jesus, who has shown Himself to be the God of their deepest longings and the only One who can deliver them.

We welcome all our visitors and missions school students, who come to us from all over the world. The needs are huge, not only in Mozambique, but in all of Africa. We are expanding into Central and North Africa, especially DR Congo and Sudan, and are always at the raw edge of our faith, finances and resources. We have a vision for taking in many thousands more children. The spiritual warfare is strong, and we ask that you pray with us for a strong shield of angelic protection.

We continue to be deeply moved and grateful for your generosity and also for the interest so many have shown in becoming involved with us. We can make good use of nearly every gift, skill and background as we build our infrastructure and send out more and more missionaries around the world. Thank you for loving us, praying for us, supporting us and being thrilled with our God along with us! We love our family in Him!

In His great love,
Rolland

Confidence in Him

> Though you have not seen Him, you love Him, and though you do not see Him now, but believe in Him, you greatly rejoice with joy inexpressible and full of glory.
>
> 1 Peter 1:8, NASB

Faith and joy are rare commodities among us but valuable and precious beyond words. How extraordinary that we chase after other things in our meetings at the expense of these. Our salvation is complete in Him, and we honor our God by not detracting from the all-sufficiency of the Gospel. In faith our desperation gives way to righteousness, peace and joy in the Holy Spirit—without measure! Our total trust in our Savior is the substance of our intimacy with Him, and no self-condemnation or weakness can diminish our fiery love affair with our God.

We trust Jesus to save us from ourselves. We trust Him to take initiative in and through us. All bright ideas come from Him, and He has no lack of them! We are set completely free from all pressure. There is no compulsion in His Kingdom.

But if we are so totally helpless without Him, how does He still enjoy our company? In Jesus we are the crowning achievement of all His creative power. We find our greatest liberty at the point of His most complete control, where we are set free by His Spirit to do what is most spectacularly, ravishingly perfect. We and our lives are the field of the activity of His mind, which we must never underestimate. We are the outcome and substance of His joy. By His Spirit we partake of His pleasure, tasting the perfection of relationship that could rise only from His infinite imagination. He delights in His own handiwork, which is our delight in Him. How perfect is our God!

We pass through repentance and tears again and again on our journey to our heavenly home, but these are not our destination. We endure for the joy set before us, the very motivation of Jesus Himself (see Hebrews 12:2). We are destined for the home of righteousness, where every tear is wiped away.

So in Africa, we miraculously maintain a positive outlook in the face of the worst Satan can do. We lower ourselves in broken humility, only to rise in the joy of the Lord, more than conquerors through Him who loved us. By taking pleasure in our God, we rout the enemy. By pursuing the free gift of holiness and refusing condemnation, we find every reason to be lighthearted.

There is still so much work to be done among the poor and lost. So much suffering and disease remain. But faltering faith will not help us face reality. We much prefer to "live in denial," reveling in what Jesus will do next among us. Hardly passive, we run the race in Him, taking hold of the promise of the Gospel in all its glory. We stay connected to the Head, carefully keeping our balance, learning to distinguish good from evil.

When down and tired, we strengthen ourselves and regain our joy by putting all our faith back in Him alone. We retreat into His heart, that safe place under His wings, that fortress in the Rock. We cannot lose. We will not be ashamed. We will see the salvation of the Lord spread through the most unstable, violent and out-of-control areas of Africa. Jesus knows how to glorify Himself and look out for His own reputation. We are unspeakably graced to participate in His work. And then we awake to new mercies and fresh motivation, never stepping away from Him and the life that flows from the vine into the branches.

In newsletter after newsletter, we have issued an invitation to join us in missions. We do that not out of desperation but in faith and love. It is to your advantage to obey the Gospel, freely and with great joy, bearing tremendous fruit. May you hear His voice clearly and respond with His energy. In our world here in Africa, we have great needs of every kind, but we look forward with huge anticipation to what Jesus will do through His Body. We are already overwhelmed by what He has been doing through all of you who have helped us in so many ways.

Please pray for us with patience and faith. We do not run ahead of the Spirit, but we try to stay sensitive to Him as we expand into new frontiers in Africa and around the world.

Much love in Jesus,
Rolland

From Heidi photos

1. Excitement before the dedication of our new village church

2. Heidi cuts the ribbon (string!) to open the new church

3. Preaching to the children

4. Our new church congregation

5. Heidi with local mamas beautified Mozambican-style

Overnight in the bush photo

Heidi and Pastor Jose with the deaf father of two (on Heidi's left), now healed

Conclusion

I'm at a "Catch the Fire" conference in the States, suddenly far removed from the mud huts and poverty of Africa where I just was. And again I see how separated the "haves" are from the "have-nots" in this country. The tension between these groups fuel most of the conflicts in the world today and is one of the main challenges of missions and the work of God on the earth.

But we are not just after redressing material imbalance. We are not even simply after church growth and increased wealth. We are after an indefinable something called "revival," lots of it, in greater and greater power, that sets on fire and makes alive every aspect of our being. We are after a revelation of Jesus Christ that undoes what the devil has done, unleashing a glory that puts us in continual awe of a Sovereign God who does not lack for initiative and is not bound by the limitations of our understanding and vision. He is not waiting for us to set Him free to work by supplying our permission, requests and ideas, but He graciously infuses us with His vision and passion until His own workmanship in us is a thrill to Him!

Knowing His sovereignty, and in the healthy fear of the Lord, we take nothing for granted. We are not passive, but with confidence that the Gospel of Jesus Christ is sufficient in every situation, we run the race to win with fiery zeal. Using all the faith and strength we have so far, we pursue not success with corporate management in missions, but the holiness without which no one will see the Lord. We pursue an irresistible power that comes only with lowliness, patience, kindness and a love that does not fail. We pursue a presence and atmosphere where intimacy kisses purity, the radical outcome of faith in the power of the cross. We pursue perfection in Jesus that results in a joy that no one and nothing in this world can diminish.

In Africa we are not trying to prop up and sustain a revival however we can; we are trying to keep up with the Holy Spirit, who is racing ahead of us, igniting hunger like wildfire in country after country. Satan tries everything he can to stop us, throwing at us crisis after crisis just when we feel we can't handle one more. We deal with every kind of corruption, immorality, thievery, jealousy, false motives, insecurity, death threats—and even witchcraft in the camp. Administratively, we are far over our heads with our little staff. Financially, we have been walking on water for years, so accountable to God that if we do not please Him and He stops supporting us miraculously even for a day, we are finished.

But we just graduated the students of our second Holy Given missions school in Pemba. Some one hundred fifty students from fifteen countries reached another spiritual climax in the cultural setting of the poorest of the poor. By day they soaked in the presence of God and the teaching of our many speakers. By night, in a stream of outreaches, together with our Mozambican pastors, they saw with their own eyes village after village coming to Jesus in response to the Kingdom breaking in upon them with undeniable supernatural power. Chiefs continue to grab our microphones and tell their Moslem villages that they will all now follow this Jesus who has proven Himself to be God. Each week the Holy Spirit keeps using Heidi, our children, our staff and our students to bring hearing to the deaf, sight to the blind and enduring hope to the lost.

Heidi especially has been given a special anointing for the deaf, and basically at every outreach she will send the people to bring their deaf from anywhere in the village, right out of their huts, even late at night, and all will receive their hearing. Every healing brings more excitement and joy and eagerness to learn all the more about this Jesus. A high point for us recently was a baptism in Pemba's beautiful ocean, when we baptized a man who could not stop grinning broadly because he had just received a great deal of his sight back after being totally blind—not even able to see faint light, looking right at the sun.

» p. 194

And so we press on to what lies ahead, not content with what we have already, but electrified with an appetite for dimensions of revival we cannot comprehend yet. Our bodies and nerves may almost fail us, but His transcendent power carries us onward and upward. Our trust in Him is a gift, our life is a gift, our joy is a gift, our anointing is a gift, our initiative is a gift. . . . We love Him because He first loved us. We run after Him alone because He will not fail us.

Who will run with us? Who will catch the fire and burn with undying passion and joy? Who has been hopelessly captured by the Holy Spirit's advances and cannot resist throwing their lives away on Jesus? Where are His fools? His friends? Who will see the world as He sees it and respond as He responds, becoming one spirit with Him? Who has caught the fire and cannot stop burning?

Urgent, hungry cries for spiritual help come to us daily—lately from Zimbabwe, Ethiopia, Zambia, Kenya, Tanzania, Rwanda and across Europe. We are weak, often tired and not excited by more and more administration alone. But we are energized by a vision of unending revival based solidly on the Gospel once and for all delivered to the saints. We are sustained not by "secrets" we have learned, but by childlike, joyful simplicity in embracing the grace of God revealed in Jesus for all to see.

Let us know if you want to help—in the Lord! We are unspeakably grateful to those who are already helping and deeply involved with us. We now look after 4,500 orphaned children—thank you for caring about the poor.

Much, much love in Jesus,
Rolland

Conclusion photo

A totally blind man, unable to see any light while staring at the sun, with most of his sight miraculously restored

About Iris Ministries

"Blessed are the poor in spirit,
for theirs is the kingdom of heaven."

Matthew 5:3

Rolland and Heidi Baker began Iris Ministries, Inc., an inter-denominational mission, in 1980 and have been missionaries for

Rolland and Heidi Baker with their daughter, Crystalyn, son, Elisha, and family dogs at home in Pemba

the past 25 years. They were both ordained as ministers in 1985 after completing their B.A. and M.A. degrees at Southern California College in biblical studies and church leadership. Rolland is a third-generation missionary, born and raised in China and Taiwan. He was greatly influenced by his grandfather, H. A. Baker, who wrote *Visions Beyond the Veil*, an account of the extended visions of heaven and hell that children received in his remote orphanage in southwest China two generations ago.

Heidi was powerfully called to the mission field when she was sixteen and living on an Indian reservation as an American Field Service student. She was led to the Lord by a Navajo preacher. Several months later she was taken up in a vision for several hours and heard the Lord speak to her and tell her to be a minister and a missionary to Africa, Asia and England. When she returned home to Laguna Beach, California, she began ministering at every opportunity and leading short-term missions teams. Rolland and Heidi met at a small charismatic church in Southern California and married six months later, after realizing they were united in their calling and desire to see revival among the poor and forgotten of the world.

Rolland and Heidi spent twelve years in Asia. The first six years they led Christian dance-drama crusades in Philippines, Taiwan, Indonesia and Hong Kong. They made use of their backgrounds in creative media and the performing arts and saw thousands come to Jesus.

After meeting Jackie Pullinger-To and working with her ministry to drug addicts in Hong Kong, however, they had a strong feeling that the Lord wanted to change the direction of their ministry. Their hearts were increasingly broken for the poor and unwanted. They wondered about their crusade converts and wanted to concentrate more on the specific daily needs of those to whom they ministered. This was a time of change. They began to plant works among the poor—first in the slums of central Jakarta, Indonesia, and then among forgotten streetsleepers and elderly in the most crowded urban area in the world, central Kowloon in Hong Kong. God was giving them His heart for the poor and abandoned.

In 1992 they left to do their Ph.D.s in systematic theology at King's College, University of London. At the same time, they planted a church among the homeless, drug addicts and alcoholics who lived on the streets in central London.

In 1995, after twenty years of praying and waiting, they arrived in Mozambique, the poorest country in the world. The government offered Iris Ministries a horribly dilapidated and neglected "orphanage," and with no promised support for such a project they simply said, "Yes, we'll take it!" They began with eighty children, but their hearts were broken for the lost and abandoned children still on the streets of Maputo. After many years of brutal civil war, thousands were left orphaned, displaced and abandoned. The Mozambican and foreign staff of Iris Ministries began to pick up and take in these lost children. God poured down His love and provided food day by day. They grew to 320 children. They planted a church in the community and began to see hundreds turn their hearts to the Lord.

The former communist directors of the government orphanage were furious ever since the Bakers took over, since their extreme corruption and thievery had been stopped. Scheming together with an equally corrupt faction of the government, they concocted accusations and issued a legal decree to Iris Ministries, forbidding prayer and worship, "Christian singing" and all forms of "unapproved" food and clothing distribution and medical assistance. If they and their children did not obey these new rules, they would have 48 hours to leave. Heidi was also told that there was a contract out on her life and that she was not allowed back on the property. Overwhelmed and exhausted by the fight, Iris Ministries had to evacuate to its office in the city.

At the center, the children entered the dining room, which had also been used as a church, and began singing praise and worship songs at the tops of their lungs! They were beaten by the people whom the authorities had appointed to take over running the center, and were told they were not allowed to worship God. One by one they began to walk the twenty miles to the city office. They told Papa Rolland and Mama Ida that they would go wherever they were, because they wanted to worship God! Not knowing what to do, they all cried out to God in total desperation. They had lost everything. There was no place for them to go. There was not even a pot to cook for all these children! Nelda Lawrence, a friend from the U.S. Embassy, came over with some chili and rice for the Baker family. Heidi said, "We have a very large family!" Nelda said, "No, this is only for you and your two children." Heidi replied, "We have a lot of children, and the Lord said there would always be enough!" They prayed over the pots of food and told the more than fifty children to sit down. Everyone ate and was full, including the Bakers!

Two other missions, hearing of the situation, offered the use of some unused buildings for three months. As the time ended, the Lord graciously provided a piece of land. The children prayed and interceded with the whole staff and believed God for another miracle. As always, God came through and provided a huge circus tent and some used army tents in which the children could live. Holes were dug for toilets, and everyone prayed for months for water from the earth (a well) and spiritual water from heaven (more of the Holy Spirit). God answered both prayers and provided a well with clean, fresh water and poured His Holy Spirit out on the children in a powerful way. Through the trials, everyone grew stronger in the Lord. The greatest joy for the whole center was that its members were now free to worship God.

The challenges of providing physically and spiritually for so many children under unspeakable conditions of poverty and evil are being met in Jesus. Time after time, as discouragement and exhaustion have threatened to collapse the entire ministry effort in

Mozambique, the Holy Spirit has poured out more grace and mercy on the ministry.

At one point Heidi came back to the States to attend a renewal conference (being in drastic need of renewal!). She was exhausted by the work and the responsibility of over three hundred children who all called her "Mama Ida." The enemy tried everything to stop her from making the trip. It looked financially impossible, and two doctors told her she absolutely could not make the trip because she had pneumonia. Stubborn as she is, she got on the plane for the thirty-some-hour journey. Mercifully, at the start of the conference God opened up her lungs and allowed her to breathe freely. Each day her strength increased. She spent many hours receiving prayer from loving people on the ministry team. It was difficult and at the same time deeply healing to simply receive after preaching and teaching for so many years. One night she felt she was in birth pains and was groaning in intercession for the children of Mozambique. In a vision she could see thousands of them coming toward her, and she cried, "No, Lord, there are too many!" She felt Jesus say, *Look into My eyes. You give them something to eat.* Then He took a piece of His broken body and it became bread, and she began to give it to the children. Then again the Lord said, *Look into My eyes. You give them something to drink.* He gave her a cup of the blood and the water that flowed from His side, and she gave this to the children to drink. The Lord spoke to her heart and said, *There will always be enough bread and drink, because I paid the price with My life. Don't be afraid. Only believe.* She returned to Mozambique, healed and strengthened.

Today, Rolland and Heidi cry out for a continuation of the visitation of God experienced by the children of H. A. Baker's orphanage in China long ago. That is beginning to happen, and more testimonies are accumulating than can be communicated. May the Word of God spread in power to the remote corners of the world, and may the poor, the crippled, the lame and the blind—people who have never before tasted the goodness of God—be drawn to the King's great banquet!

Now, Iris Ministries has expanded to more than six thousand churches all over Mozambique and into neighboring countries. The disastrous flooding of 2000/2001 catalyzed an overwhelming hunger for the things of God in the refugee camps where Iris ministered, and the Gospel continues to spread like wildfire. Iris now cares for almost 4,500 children at its centers, and its churches are taking in orphans as well. Jesus is revealing Himself through signs and wonders, visions and dreams, and Iris has never seen such a harvest. May the Lord of the harvest send workers!

About Iris Ministries photos

1. Heidi with some of our younger children at our house

2. Giving our children ice cream at the beach

3. Our new and happy family in Pemba, always growing

4. Congo 2006: Our first rented church building and headquarters

5. Congo 2006: Beginning a Kalonge worship service in our new church

6. Congo 2006: Stuck in the mud, again

7. Congo: One of our Kalonge boys—innocence and joy

Contacting Iris Ministries

Rolland and Heidi Baker, directors:
Iris Ministries, Inc.
P.O. Box 275
Pemba, Cabo Delgado
Mozambique
Tel: +258-82-303-0680
rolland@irismin.org
heidi@irismin.org
(For mail and small packages only, not donations.
Checks must be returned to the U.S.A. for deposit.)

U.S. mail and support:
Iris Ministries, Inc.
P.O. Box 493995
Redding, CA 96049-3995
USA
Tel: 530-255-2077
irisredding@earthlink.net

Missions school:
Information and online applications: www.irismin.com
Graduates: graduates@irismin.org

Visitor inquiries (dates, travel, preparation, etc.):
hospitality@irismin.org

Pemba inquiries:
pemba@irismin.org

Website:
www.irismin.org
(past newsletters, photos, online donations and blog, info for wire-transfer donations)

Administrative website:
www.irismin.com
(ministry locations, products, itineraries, online donations, contact and support, long-term service, visiting Iris, Holy Given missions school information and online applications, latest news and missionary contact information)

Inquiries regarding container shipments, needs and logistics:
Gordon Haggerty
ghaggerty@attglobal.net

Malawi contact:
David and Joanna Morrison
Partners In Harvest—Iris Africa
P.O. Box 2379, Blantyre
Malawi
Landline in Bangula: +265-1-453-368
Cell: +265-8-343-814
mo@globemw.net

Los Angeles fax and voice mail:
(will be converted and sent to us by email)
+1-213-330-0293

Addresses for packages of donated goods sent by surface mail:

Iris Ministries, Inc.
P.O. Box 20017
West Acres 1211
Nelspruit, South Africa

(For mail and small packages only, not donations.
Checks must be returned to the U.S.A. for deposit.)

Iris Ministries Canada
3092 Shannon Crescent
Oakville, ON L6L 6B4
Canada
Tel: 905-847-7749; fax: 905-847-7931
www.irismin.ca
info@irismin.ca
Contact Janis Chevreau, director

(Donations from Canada can go to this address for tax receipts.)

Iris Ministries (UK) Ltd.
P.O. Box 351
Tonbridge, Kent TN9 1WQ
United Kingdom
info@irisministries.co.uk
www.irisministries.co.uk

(Donations from the U.K. can go to this address for tax receipts.)

ALWAYS ENOUGH:
God's Miraculous Provision among the Poorest Children on Earth

Even the most desperate poverty, the most devastating illness, the most heart-wrenching grief is not beyond God's help. His love and power have no limits—and that's a message readers from all walks of life need to hear. The modern miracles that Rolland and Heidi Baker experience every day in their work with Mozambique's throwaway children, movingly chronicled in *Always Enough*, will inspire anyone looking for hope in the midst of suffering.

The Bakers, formerly missionaries in Indonesia and Hong Kong, share how their work for the past eight years in Mozambique, one of the poorest nations on earth, has borne spiritual fruit beyond their wildest dreams. Every day presents multiple impossible needs. But in the face of everything Satan can do, as Rolland and Heidi lay down their lives and "minister to the one," there is always enough.

Readers will discover that the simple practice of choosing to step out and trust God every day unleashes His provision for every need.

Praise for ALWAYS ENOUGH

"What God has done through the anointing of His Spirit in the lives of Rolland and Heidi Baker is truly miraculous. I know of no other work so pure and so motivated by the compassionate heart of God. This is not only the story of how God would take fourteen people and one church and grow it in five years to more than six thousand churches. It the story of how God would prepare His chosen instruments for the powerful faith-based ministry that is presently shaking twelve countries in southern Africa."

—Randy Clark, Global Awakening

Chosen *Spirit-Filled Living* a division of Baker Publishing Group • www.chosenbooks.com